The impact that Dolly Parton made on the field of popular music was felt strongly in 1978, the year when Dolly captured three Broadcast Music Incorporated country awards, proof positive that she hadn't lost her country fans while crossing over into mainstream music. The American Guild of Variety Artists named Dolly Parton Best Female Country Performer of the Year, and she won the top honor in the music business, her first Grammy Award, for Best Female Country Vocalist Performance on a single, thanks to "Here You Come Again."

But, more important than any of these, 1978 was the year when Dolly was handed what she had always prayed for; in October, at the Country Music Association's twelfth annual presentation telecast from Nashville, Dolly Parton was voted not merely Best *Female* Entertainer, but Entertainer of the Year, the single highest award that the CMA can bestow. Dolly's cup was overflowing with self-righteous happiness; she could ask for no better confirmation that her hotly disputed career moves had been wise decisions.

*Dolly*

# *Dolly*
# *HERE I COME AGAIN*

## Leonore Fleischer

A STAR BOOK
published by
the Paperback Division of
W.H. Allen & Co. Plc

A Star Book
Published in 1988
by The Paperback Division of
W. H. Allen & Co. Plc
44 Hill Street, London W1X 8LB

First published in the United States of America by
PaperJacks Ltd, New York, 1987

Copyright © 1987 by Leonore Fleischer

Printed and bound in Great Britain by
Anchor Brendon Ltd, Tiptree, Essex

ISBN 0 352 32190 3

# TABLE OF CONTENTS

"If I could get their attention long enough, I felt they would see beneath the boobs and find the heart, and that they would see beneath the wig and find the brains. I think one big part of whatever appeal I possess is the fact that I look totally one way and that I am totally another. I look artificial, but I'm not."

—Dolly Parton, in a 1981 interview with *Los Angeles Times* writer Robert Hilburn

# *Dolly*
## HERE I COME AGAIN

# *Prologue*

**Rags to Rhinestones**

> So what do you think? Are they
> as big as you thought they were
> going to be?
>
> —Dolly Parton

Seen from the audience, even in her 5-inch
heels and her towering blond wig, Dolly Parton
looks small, almost fragile, which is strange when
one considers (as everybody does) her interna-
tionally famous physical endowments, possibly
the most talked-about, written-about, joked-about
pair of flotation devices since Jane Russell's.
There's at least one major difference between Dolly
Parton and Jane Russell, though. Jane's boobs were
an integral part of her smoldering sexuality. Her

1

cleavage in *The Outlaw* was the promise of more, much more, to come. Dolly's boobs are . . . cheerful. Rather than sexy, they are a country-style exaggeration of good-natured abundance, a gift from a jolly deity poking fun.

Dolly herself makes jokes about her voluptuous figure. One of her favorites is, "The reason my feet are so tiny is that things don't grow in the shade." Often, she'll kid her audience. "Ah see you out there with your binoculars, and Ah know jes' what you're lookin' at. But what you didn't realize is that you didn't need your binoculars."

These days she's very thin, having recently lost fifty pounds; her backside is tiny, her waistline measures Scarlett O'Hara's size, 18 inches, but her breasts are still . . . Dolly's breasts. "When I try to do pushups, they never leave the floor," she quips, with a playful wink at her fans. She has always refused to reveal her bust measurement, but swears it's nowhere near the 45 inches that the press has estimated, pointing out that she's only 5 feet tall and has a small frame.

And here's a paradox: On the one hand, Dolly Parton dresses to show off those celebrated mammaries; on the other, she is constantly complaining, in person and in print, that people don't look beneath the breasts to find her heart.

But then Dolly herself is something of a paradox, this curvaceous woman with the sweet, dimpled face and breathy voice of a little girl, this God-loving country woman dressed like a city siren, powdered and painted, bespangled, besequined, bewigged, this 5-foot woman who is a creative songwriter, a great performer, the person listed in *The Guinness Book of World Records* as the highest-paid female entertainer in the world, a shrewd business entrepreneur who not only owns her own music publishing and film production companies, but her very own theme park!

Dolly Parton has taken a unique composite of country shrewdness, innocence, full-figured sensuality, and backwoods gospel-singing fervor and built it into a public persona that reaches across the footlights and takes the listener by the hand. "Howdy," she seems to say with every song. "Come set a spell." On the screen she sparkles with personality; her image comes across fresh and clean, despite the outlandishly vulgar clothing, clanking jewelry, and often preposterous trademark wigs. Even when she played a madam in *The Best Little Whorehouse in Texas*, she exuded a breath of mountain air and a healthy freshness.

Having traveled the long road from a backwoods dirt farm in the foothills of the Great Smoky Mountains to become one of the superstars of the entertainment world, Dolly earns millions of dollars and gives money away with a free and generous hand. As much as she is paid, she's worth more, because every bone in her little body is making that effort to please the people who flock to see her, to see them go away smiling.

Her small hands, covered in gold and diamond rings, strike chords on the guitar, and that famous voice swells out through the microphone to capture the audience with its sweet vibrato. On one finger, a ring revolves to catch the light. Made of diamonds to Dolly's own design, the ring features twin butterflies, one behind the other, that pivot and spin when her hands move, catching the light like a precious pinwheel. Dolly loves butterflies; she has taken the butterfly as kind of a personal symbol and wears the representation of one at all times. Their beauty and freedom, the bright colors of their wings, are a mirror of her own personality. Besides, she can't resist anything bright and sparkling.

When Dolly Parton began to sing professionally, she was paid $20 a week, which wasn't bad money for a ten-year-old. Today she is forty-one, and ABC-TV has just signed her to a record $40,000,000 contract for a new series of variety spectaculars, and the network has committed to thirteen shows. When she plays Las Vegas, she commands close to $500,000 a week. In her career, she's won three Grammy Awards; among her more than 60 albums are five gold and three platinum; she's had 22 number-one hit singles. Dolly has gathered up into her small hands, with their long red nails, every award a performer can win, including being voted Entertainer of the Year by the Country Music Association. She's won many awards two or three times. *People* magazine once wrote that Dolly Parton "ought to be declared a national treasure."

Her crossover from country to the pop charts was one of the few successful such transitions in the music business. Dolly went from the cover of *Country Music* to the cover of *Rolling Stone* without a backward glance. More than once, she's graced the cover of *People*. She moved from the top of the country charts to the top of the pop charts without losing her down-home flavor or her down-home fans. Her legion of worshippers just grew larger.

For all her wigs and spangles, her elaborate dresses, false eyelashes, 3-inch blood-red acrylic fingernails, vulgar jewelry, and a Mae West figure, this is no floozy, no bimbo, no dumb blonde. She is the author of more than 3,000 songs. She is the witty, intelligent, down-to-earth woman whom the feminist magazine *Ms.* selected as one of its 1986 Women of the Year, for "creating popular songs about real women," and for "bringing jobs and understanding to the mountain people of Tennessee." Once again, the paradox.

What makes up the Dolly Parton magic? What drives her to work so hard, even in the face of illness and exhaustion? In a world where talent often goes unrewarded, how did Dolly rise to the very top of the heap? She didn't claw her way there; she didn't cheat her way there. She worked harder and longer than most others would have done without becoming discouraged. She did it on her own, with determination, grit, cheerful optimism, and, above all, deep faith in the Lord. Where others despair, Dolly Parton dreams; where others curse, Dolly Parton prays.

But as she traveled that long, exhausting road, what tolls did she have to pay? To gain what she has, what was she forced to surrender? What did she lose along the way? Nobody's life, no matter how privileged or sheltered, is free of pain. Nobody makes it to the top of the heap without changing, without sacrificing something too secret and too precious to name. What are Dolly Parton's secrets?

# Chapter One

## Make a Joyful Noise Unto the Lord

I was born with a happy nature and a happy heart. I was born with the gift of understanding people and loving them and I've never been unhappy. I've always seen the light at the end of the tunnel.

—Dolly Parton

When you think of Tennessee, you think of music. Just the mention of the name brings to mind Beale Street, Memphis, home of the blues, of W. C. Handy and the moanin' low of rich black voices. When you say "Tennessee" you say Elvis Presley the King, and Graceland, the 15,000-square-foot palace where he once reigned supreme and still does, even in death. When you think of

Tennessee, Nashville comes immediately to mind—
the "Grand Ole Opry" and the entertainment and
recording empire built by country music pickers
and singers. And, when you think of Tennessee,
you have to think of Dolly Parton.

The sovereign state of Tennessee in all its natural glory was once the property of the Cherokee
Indians. Its very name comes from the Cherokee
name *Tanasi*. Even today, one can still see traces
of the Cherokee Indian beauty in the faces of
some Tennesseans—the straight, black glossy hair,
the high cheekbones and dark slanting eyes, often
combined with the fairer features of the Irish,
Scottish, and English farmers and settlers who
came in the 1700s to fight the French and the
Indians and take possession of the land.

Eastern Tennessee, near the North Carolina
border, is a world of forests and mountains, of
rivers and national parks and wildlife preserves.
When spring arrives at the foothills of the Great
Smoky Mountains, the wild dogwood trees come
into flower, as though millions of fragile white
butterflies had settled on their branches for just
a little while. Long rows of budding forsythia
bushes are heavy with golden flowers echoing
the color of the sun. Azaleas and massive rho-
dodendrons, which thrive in the acid soil beneath the tall evergreens, burst into a dazzling
display of flowering, setting the hollows of the
hills and the fertile reddish bottomland ablaze
with crimson and purple. The pink-and-white
blossoms of the mountain laurel blanket the
hillsides, casting delicate shadows like lace over
the harsh outcroppings of granite. Hickory trees

and elms, slender poplars and sturdy oaks, fragrant pine and cedar dig their roots in deep and hold the land, spreading canopies of their leaves over the hollows and the ridges.

In springtime, Sevier County in eastern Tennessee appears lush with promise. Along the Little Pigeon River the daffodils and wild wood hyacinth come early into their bloom. But the soil of the remote hillsides in the backwoods country is often thin and rocky, and it can be mighty hard to scratch a decent living out of it.

It was into this magnificent contradiction— earth's beauty masking the hard work, hard times, and doing without—that a baby girl was born on a snowy morning, January 19, 1946, just on the cusp between Capricorn and Aquarius. She drew her first breath and hollered her first musical holler in a Locust Ridge, Sevier County, backwoods two-room cabin.

Her daddy and mama were Robert Lee and Avie Lee Parton. They named the baby Dolly Rebecca; she was the first of the Parton children to inherit her father's light coloring.

"Daddy's people are fair and blond and blue-eyed," Dolly was to tell the world in later years. "My mama's people have a lot of Indian blood, so they're dark, with high cheekbones and real dark hair. I have Mama's features, Mama's smile, and her dimples, but I got my daddy's nose. I also got my pride and determination from Daddy, but I got my mama's personality."

Lee Parton had no cash to pay Dr. Robert F. Thomas, who delivered his daughter, so they paid him in kind—some cornmeal ground from corn Lee had grown himself. "That's what I cost," a smiling Dolly would proudly tell reporters after she became famous, "a sack o' cornmeal."

Dolly Parton came into this world just at the end of the hot war and the beginning of the Cold War, at the very dawning of the postwar atomic age, only five months after American bombings leveled Hiroshima and Nagasaki, thus bringing the war to a hideous end and introducing the human race to the annihilistic powers of the atom bomb.

Sevier County is not far from Oak Ridge, Tennessee, where American scientists and engineers had labored to bring to birth the era of nuclear technology. Yet, ironically, the backwoods mountain country of Tennessee would move very slowly into the modern age, just as it had remained virtually untouched by the war, with the exception of the young mountain men who had died or been maimed in the fighting.

In other parts of the South, women had moved from the farms into the cities to take on men's work when menfolk had put on uniforms and gone off to serve their country. It was one of the great American societal shifts of the twentieth century, the population change from rural to urban, and women entering the workplace in force, never to leave it again. They would never again be kept down on the farm once they'd seen a paycheck.

But in the hills where Dolly was born, on the virtual back porch of the house where the atom bomb was built, life was still very much the same

10

as it had been before the war. Menfolk sowed and harvested the crops, and did the heaviest chores; women raised the babies and did practically everything else that needed doing on a farm. There were no electrical appliances in the Parton household, at least until the girls grew up enough to help their mother cook, clean, and look after the little ones. Sons and daughters were the only labor-saving devices mountain families had.

Dolly was the fourth Parton child, fourth in a dirt-poor but fiercely independent family that would number twelve children, eleven of whom lived to grow up. When their oldest, Willadeene, was born about a year after her parents' wedding, Avie Lee was but sixteen. When Dolly Rebecca came kicking and hollering into the world—although her family says she was born singing— her mother was only twenty-two. It's hard to get more country than that—a rural mountain cabin in the South, poor dirt farmers, kids coming year after year, and parents not much older than other folks' brothers and sisters.

"Mama grew up with us kids," Dolly would joke to the world years later. "There was always one on her and one in her." And it was true. First came Willadeene, then David and Denver; next, Dolly Rebecca, the last Parton baby to be born at home. After her, Avie Lee always went to a clinic or to the hospital, and there she gave birth to Bobby, Stella, Cassie, Randy, and Larry. Because Avie Lee suffered a life-threatening attack of spinal meningitis when she was carrying Larry, the baby lived for only nine hours after he was born.

But the family never forgot him. "We were twelve kids," they always say, which still includes Larry.

Floyd and Frieda, the twins, were next in line, and after the twins came Rachel, the youngest. All the children shared a mixed Dutch, Irish, and Cherokee heritage that is truly melting-pot America.

Avie Lee Owens, with her Indian cheekbones and silky raven hair, was fifteen years old on the day Robert Lee Parton, called Lee, first set eyes on her and fell in love. He was seventeen, with reddish-blond coloring inherited from his ancestors in the British Isles. He saw her in church; she was the preacher's daughter, and he made his mind up there and then to marry that pretty Avie Lee. Even by mountain people's standards they were very young to marry, but they were a determined pair, and two days later they were man and wife. That was almost fifty years ago, and they are still like bride and groom today, still deeply in love.

Life in those days was a struggle; although Lee Parton was an unlettered man who could neither read nor write, he was "the smartest man I've ever known," as Dolly praised him. Hard-working, independent, and proud, he rose before dawn every morning to pull a meager existence out of the ground. When crops failed, or when the harvest was in, he would hire himself out as a construction worker, carpenter, or day laborer to support his rapidly growing family. In the early years of their marriage, Lee made and sold moonshine whiskey out of corn mash; it was an illegal activity, because moonshine carried no revenue tax stamps, but it was hardly an uncommon practice in the hills. When Avie Lee, the preacher's daughter, disapproved, her husband gave up moonshining to please her.

But, hard as the couple worked, the kids kept coming and Avie Lee was often ill. The spinal meningitis she had when carrying Larry nearly killed her; her fever was so high that she had to be packed in ice. The doctor gave her up for lost, telling the stricken family that, even if Mama lived, she would be a cripple for life. But, just like a miracle, the following morning there was Avie Lee, sitting up in bed and smiling. Nevertheless, the illness took its toll on her strength and left her deaf in one ear.

In between the childbirths there were miscarriages that further sapped Avie Lee's energies. In her song "In the Good Ole Days When Times Were Bad," Dolly would later immortalize those difficult days. No amount of money could buy those years from her, she would write, and no amount of money could pay her to go back and live them over again.

"In a big country family," Dolly would tell interviewer Cliff Jahr years later, "you're just brought up by the hair of her head. You do what you got to. I—believe it or not—was a tomboy. I could climb a tree or wrestle or run as fast as any brother. We faced starvation, but Mama and Daddy taught values you don't learn in schoolrooms— God, nature, how to care for other people and for the land, how to trust people and when not to. In a way, I'm still that little stringy-headed girl who ran around barefoot, sores on her legs, fever blisters, no clothes, who dreamed of being someone special someday."

The kids slept three or four, sometimes more, in crude beds, with no sheets, only stitched-together rags. "As soon as I'd go to bed," Dolly remembers, "the kids would wet on me. That was the only warm thing we knew in the wintertime. That was our most pleasure—to get peed on. If you could just not fan the cover. If you kept the air out from under the cover, the pee didn't get so cold."

In winter, the Parton kids would bundle up in clothing before going to bed, and huddle together for warmth.

Since there wasn't a hope of indoor plumbing in the cabin, and the outdoor plumbing consisted of little more than a one-holer, a tiny shack hiding a hole cut in a board over a limepit, well-worn by generations of backsides, with cut-up donated newspapers for toilet paper, how did the Parton family bathe? It was a question that Lawrence Grobel would ask Dolly in his famous *Playboy* interview in 1978.

"We made our own soap," replied Dolly, "and in the summertime, we'd go to the river. That was like a big bath. And we'd all go in swimming and wash each other's hair. Soap was just flowin' down the river and we were so dirty we left a ring around the Little Pigeon River."

And in the winter? "I had to take a bath every night, 'cause the kids peed on me every night. We just had a pan of water and we'd wash down as far as possible, and we'd wash up as far as possible. Then, when somebody'd clear the room, we'd wash *possible*."

Yet, even if the Partons had none of the "luxuries" that to most Americans are necessities—running water, flush toilets, decent clothes for school—even if there wasn't an extra penny to buy the things children dream about when they see pictures in someone else's old magazines or in the Sears Roebuck "wish book," even when crops were poor and there was only one hog a year to butcher for two grownups and eleven children and the kids went to bed fed only on starches with no meat, they never went hungry for affection.

"We got no money, but we're rich in love," wrote Dolly later in "Poor Folks Town." She took this saying from her mother; it was a favorite of hers. "We're rich people because we know we got love and we got each other," Dolly's mama always said. Love there was aplenty, along with Avie Lee's famous Stone Soup.

When crops failed and there were only a few vegetables in the house—potatoes, onions, maybe a few greens and tomatoes—Avie Lee Parton would send her children out to find the biggest, smoothest stones they could find. Then she would choose the best stone to add to the pot.

"Mama made such a big ole fuss about pickin' out the right one," remembers Dolly. "She'd laugh and say, 'Oh, there's magic in *this* one. I kin feel it.'"

In that way, Avie Lee passed her love, her sense of imagination and wonder, along to her children. It was a gift no amount of money could buy. "Some people may think we were real poor, but I can't see it that way," says Avie Lee Owens Parton. "We were just ordinary Americans, and I was always real proud of what we had."

Because their mother was ill so much of the time, worn out with childbearing and fevers, the older children looked after the young ones. Willadeene, Dolly, and Stella each had a "baby" of her own to look after; Dolly's was to have been Larry, but he died a few hours after birth.

"Oh, that really hurt me deep, 'cause I was at that age where I took things so hard." Dolly was only ten when Larry died—"ten years old, just tryin' to grow up and be a child at the same time." The whole family mourned the baby for a long time.

The Partons moved around a lot in search of more room, better farmland, and a more comfortable life. When Dolly was three, they moved to a tar-paper shack on a farm of several hundred acres between Locust Ridge and Webb Mountain, in the Great Smokies. There they stayed for five years, while Dolly's daddy grew a small cash crop of tobacco and food to feed his growing family, taking out the most the stony earth would allow. This was Dolly Parton's "Tennessee Mountain Home," the subject of one of her most popular country songs. A picture of the shack is on the cover of the *Tennessee Mountain Home* album, her first concept album, and possibly the first concept album in country music history. Naturally, the price of the shack itself has skyrocketed because Dolly Parton has made it so famous.

In Dollywood, the 400-acre, $6,000,000 theme

park tucked into the Great Smoky Mountains just outside Pigeon Forge that she opened in 1986, Dolly has reproduced that Webb Mountain shack, complete in every detail right down to the brass spittoon, the old foot-pedal sewing machine (the original shack had no electricity), and the sepia photograph of Lee's daddy, Luther Parton.

But actually growing up there, running barefoot, keeping the kerosene lantern burning all night so the rats wouldn't run over the bed where she was sleeping—to this day the grownup Dolly still sleeps with a light on—was often a lot less picturesque than the custom-built amusement park replica would indicate. Not to mention that, ironically, the replica most have cost a fortune to build—possibly a hundred times more than the original, and the same amount of money that was spent on the replica Dollywood cabin would have made the *real* Parton family cabin comfortable while the kids were growing up. But that's America.

"We had nothin'," Dolly told *New York Times* writer Chris Chase, "so far as material things. If you had a nice sweater or a lipstick, in our mind you had to be rich. We were so small all at once, and my daddy didn't have money to buy things." She went on to enumerate the things that entranced her as a child—flowers, birds, butterflies, junk jewelry, anything that was brightly colored or caught the light.

"When my daddy used to plow the fields, and the sun would shine down, that quartz stuff would glisten, and I was sure we had struck diamonds. I used to pick up all kinds of glass and shiny rock. I just loved the beauty of the things, the sparkle."

Dolly is still attracted to sparkle and bright colors. She once furnished her Nashville mansion with valuable antiques, as many wealthy people in the South do. "You know, everybody in Nashville collects antiques. And when we first got our house, I bought a bunch of old stuff, too. I didn't like it, it was just too drab. I like things a little more gaudy."

So Dolly got rid of all that costly antique furniture, preferring more "cheerful" and colorful brand-new pieces.

If they didn't have much in the way of material wealth, the ever-increasing Parton family had one of God's greatest gifts—the gift of music. Both sides of the family, the Owenses and the Partons, were musical, and just about all the children inherited at least some talent for it, even if none of them was to prove quite as gifted as Dolly.

"My mama's people were all of 'em singers and musicians, even songwriters. My daddy's kinfolk were musical, too. But mostly they sang at home or in the church; nobody ever thought of venturin' out of the hills and the hollers. But I was always full of dreams and plans, and I was the one had the grit to do it," states Dolly.

Grandpa Jake Owens, the hellfire reverend, wrote hundred of songs and hymns, some of which, such as "Singing His Praises," were recorded by Kitty Wells, then the acknowledged Queen of Country Music, who was most famous for "It Wasn't God Who Made Honky Tonk Angels." Years later, Dolly would record her granddaddy's song "Book of Life." Avie Lee composed songs, too,

18

and knew many folk ballads that she would sing to her children in the family "singalongs."

Even before she could talk, Dolly could hum little tunes and she was always on key. At the age of eighteen months, she was hearing little melodies in her head and humming them, unaware that they were original. Soon, she was putting simple lyrics of her own devising to the melodies. Dolly began writing complete songs by the time she was five, earlier than she learned to read and write.

"I had this little doll, and it was only made out of a corncob, and Daddy made a little wig for her out of corn silk, you know, with the tassel? I called the doll Little Tiny Tassel-Top, and I made up a little song about her. I was five years old."

It was at that age that Dolly first realized the songs she hummed were her own, because it was then that she went to her mother and asked her, "Mama, will you write this song down for me?" And she sang "Little Tiny Tassel-Top" for Avie Lee.

To this day Dolly Parton can't read a note of music. When she writes a song, she sings it into a tape recorder and then sends it out to a professional service to have the music transcribed onto music paper. But even back then music flowed naturally from the little girl with the rosy cheeks, the bright blue eyes, and the deep dimples. Her grandfather, the Reverend Jake Owens, said that "Dolly started singin' as soon as she quit cryin'."

"I used to make up songs and my mama would write 'em down for me," says Dolly. She said I was makin' up songs *before* I was five, but by the time I reached that age I used to beg her to write 'em down so she could read 'em back to me. When I was about seven years old, I started playin' the git-tar. It's all I've ever known."

Actually, Dolly's "git-tar" was little more than "a busted-up ol' mandolin" that was fitted out with two guitar strings. Primitive and limited as it was, to Dolly it was a genuine musical instrument and she wrote many songs with only its few chords.

"Music was a freedom," Dolly told Toby Thompson of *The Village Voice* in 1976. "My mama's people all picked some musical instruments and sung. Most of my daddy's people did." Her heritage of song came from gospel music, from the Church of God assembly, Avie Lee's father's little backwoods church, where everyone would gather together to "make a joyful noise unto the Lord."

"I been makin' a joyful noise ever since." Dolly laughs. The Parton kids' granddaddy, the Reverend Jake Owens, is the hero of Dolly's song entitled "Daddy Was an Old-Time Preacher Man," and he preached a hellfire-and-brimstone sermon. In Dolly's words, "He preached hell so hot you could feel the heat." Before and after the scripture readings and the sermon, the congregation would sing. The faithful would bring their country instruments—fiddles, tambourines, guitars, banjos, mandolins—into the church to give God praise with their picking. And they sang the simple but powerful strains of gospel hymns and old-time spirituals, which has been perhaps the strongest musical influence on Dolly Parton to this day. From the age of six, Dolly would sing her heart out in that old country church, sing the hymn tunes she loved, first with her sisters and her granddaddy, and later solo, her sweet childish soprano soaring to the wooden rafters of the little church.

The Church of God was a very free church. Aside from the scripture reading and the sermon, there was no structured service for the worshippers. "If anybody wanted to get up and sing or shout out an emotion," says Dolly, "they would do it. There was freedom there, so I came to know what freedom is, so I could know God and come to know freedom within myself." She would always associate this freedom with making music.

"I think that the soul feeling I get in my voice started with my church-singing days. The same feeling and sincerity leak over into anything I sing now."

Thanks in part to Avie Lee's deep religious faith, the family sang church hymns at home, too, accompanied by Lee Parton's banjo and guitar. But there were also "play-party" folk songs like "Old Joe Clark" and variations on the old Elizabethan ballads brought from the mother country, usually mournful songs of young men and women dying of blighted love. It was a rich, if mixed, legacy of music. Soon, Dolly was singing solo again, at home as well as in church. The child, nicknamed "Blossom" by the family ("That's gonna be the title of my autobiography, *Blossom*," vows Dolly), sang constantly, at work and at play, either hymns or the songs she had made up herself, songs about her life with her family on the farm, about sick children dying and going to Jesus, and other facets of her own experience.

Although after she had achieved success Dolly could joke about her family's poverty, her growing-up years were not an easy time for any of the Partons. "Sure we had plumbin' where I grew up. Out back! You heard o' four rooms and a bath. Our house had four rooms and a *path*! Out on Locust Ridge, the way you could tell a rich family from a poor family is that the rich family had a two-holer, and the poor family had a one-holer. We had runnin' water—that is, when one of us ran to get some. Whenever company came, Mama would say, 'Run out an' sweep the yard.' With all them children runnin' around, we didn't have no grass left out front, just a plain dirt yard, but Mama always wanted it kept nice. We'd sweep it out slick as a mole."

In the backyard, the Partons kept their vegetable garden, a pumpkin patch; they also raised some potatoes, corn, beans, turnips, greens, and other vegetables for their scanty table.

"We canned a lot. Never had much meat, mostly beans and taters. Plus biscuits and gravy. We were never really hungry, except for variety. I still love biscuits and gravy."

You can take the girl out of the country, but you can't take the country out of the girl. "When we was kids on Locust Ridge," Dolly would tell *People* magazine in a 1986 cover story, "we would always drink out of a tin can. And I still do. It seems to keep things colder. Even at my beautiful homes, I'm always drinking out of a tin can, which drives my secretary nuts. I'm saving coffee cans to drink out of and she's throwing them out and it makes me so mad. I still like to pee off the porch every now and then. There's nothing like peeing on those snobs in Beverly Hills." Dolly Parton's honest earthiness puts the Beverly Hillbillies in the shade!

The true mark of the artist is the ability to take the sad things of life and transform them into art; even more so, to take a catastrophe befalling one and weave it magically into something that can reach out and touch *millions*. Dolly Parton does this time and time again, using the raw material of her own childhood, a childhood of poverty, affection, and early dreams, but nowhere does she do it more artistically or touchingly than in one of her most beloved songs, her tribute to Avie Lee Parton's goodness and loving heart, "Coat of Many Colors." This is the song of which Dolly says, "This means more to me than any song I wrote."

The never-forgotten episode behind the song goes back to the time when Dolly was ten years old, and owned no new clothing to wear to school, only patched-up and shabby hand-me-downs. Until Dolly was nine, the Parton children attended a one-room country school, where shabbiness was universal, and nobody made fun of anybody else. But the little schoolhouse burned down, and Dolly and her brothers and sisters were forced to transfer in the middle of the term to a different school, new and modern, where the children all had unpatched and unshabby clothing to wear. The Parton children were immediately set apart, not only because of their hand-me-down clothing, but because they brought their lunches to school in paper sacks since they were unable to afford school cafeteria food.

Dolly's song says, "I didn't have a coat and it was way down in the fall." Wanting to give her daughter something new to wear to school, and mindful of Dolly's favorite Bible story about Joseph's coat of many colors, Avie Lee stitched together a coat of bright-colored corduroy scraps out of "a box of rags that someone gave us" for her little girl.

It's a story that Dolly would tell often. "Mama worked hard for weeks makin' that coat out of whatever material she could find, because she wanted me to look real nice. They were takin' our picture at school for the first time. She'd tell me how Joseph had a coat of many colors just like the one she was sewin' for me. When I put it on, I was so proud of it; I thought it was just beautiful! I thought I looked exactly like Joseph in the Bible! But when I got to school, all the other kids laughed at me and pointed their fingers.

"Rag Top! they hollered. 'Hey, you, Rag Top!' And they grabbed at my coat and pulled it until the buttons started poppin'.

"I kep' tellin' them, 'No! This is a coat of many colors, just like Joseph had in the Bible.' But they just made mock and went on yellin', 'It's just a buncha stitched-together rags!' "

Dolly didn't have a shirt or anything on under the coat, and her young breasts were just beginning to bud. The tugging at her buttons was the ultimate humiliation, and when the camera clicked for the class picture in the schoolhouse,

Dolly Parton's anguished face was captured on film, stained with tears. The episode haunts her to this day.

"I was just so ashamed I wanted to die! It was years before I could even talk to anyone about what happened."

But she fought the taunting children like a tiger. "It was one of those times when you fight to survive. Even with all the shame I felt, them kids couldn't make me not be proud of my coat of many colors."

When Dolly came home from school crying, her mother gathered her up in her arms and tried to console her. "They can only see with their eyes," she told her daughter. "But you can see with your heart."

Possibly because of painful experiences like the one with Joseph's coat, the things that always attracted Dolly as a child and to this day were luxuries the family could never afford. Somehow the little five-year-old girl took the notion that if she could write enough songs and sell them, she would have the money to buy all the pretty things she wanted, but even given those long-ago fantasies of stardom and great wealth, nobody could have foreseen just how true those dreams would come. Not even Dolly herself could have dreamed that one day she'd become the highest-paid female entertainer in the world.

There was another, even more important impetus behind Dolly's dreams other than mere pretty luxuries. She wanted to become rich so she could give her parents an easy life. Seeing her mother ill so often, and the family unable to afford doctors or decent medical care; watching her father bend his back and work until his hands cracked open and bled; seeing him injured and limping as the result of a construction accident—these tore at the young girl's tender sensibilities. If she were rich, Mama and Daddy could live comfortably and well, having all the luxuries they could never before afford. Dolly vowed that someday she would provide handsomely for her parents, and she has fulfilled that promise many times over. As soon as she had earned enough money, she bought her mama and daddy the comfortable home she always dreamed they would have. In fact, they live in a mansion high on a hill ("It's just like a Hallmark card," says Dolly), even though they still do their shopping at the local grocery store.

When she and her husband, Carl, built their 23-room dream house outside Nashville, Dolly had a special mobile home set up nearby to house her parents when they came to visit and to give them some privacy.

But that was far into the future. When Dolly was little, not only her dreams but her make-do's took the place of reality. Like most little girls, Dolly was fascinated by women's makeup, but the Partons were too poor to afford even a lipstick. "A lipstick looked like a million dollars to me," Dolly says, laughing. Avie Lee was a lenient, forgiving mother who was growing up alongside her children and who allowed them certain leeway in their activities, because she was sensitive to how her children, especially the girls, felt.

But Robert Lee Parton was a strict father who didn't hold with girls painting their faces. He never hesitated to back up his disapproval with "a whippin', but the whippin' was worth it for a few days with a red mouth." Even so, the Parton sisters often "made do," experimenting with whatever homegrown ingredients they could lay their hands on—flour for face powder, burned matches to get the carbon to darken their eyebrows, mercurochrome or merthiolate to color their lips instead of the lipstick they couldn't afford. The good thing about merthiolate was that it took a long time to wear off, so Dolly had "lipstick" on for a week or more. The medicine might have stung, but Dolly never minded. "Daddy could never rub *that* off.

"I knew I wanted to be a singer from the time when I was seven or eight and learned my first chord on the guitar. I also wanted to be a star— the biggest in the world. I wanted pretty clothes and attention and to live in a big house and buy things for Mama and Daddy. Of course, I didn't have better sense in those days.

"But as I got older, I didn't lose track of my dreams. I just thought, *Well, why can't I do all that?* The secret was to take one step at a time. And that's what I've done." Although Dolly is modest about the direct, simple way she went about obtaining her heart's desire, there is little doubt that the secret of her success lies in her spunk, her country grit, and her down-to-earth courage.

At a very early age, the precocious Dolly made up her mind that someday she'd leave the harsh and painful realities of poverty on Locust Ridge and travel the 200 miles to Nashville. There she would become a country singing star like Patsy Cline or Kitty Wells, and her dreams would all come true. Dolly never doubted those dreams. Her mother was her chief supporter, her biggest fan, and truest believer, her most constant source of encouragement. "Mama never let us lose our hopes."

Meanwhile, all Dolly could do was pick out a couple of thin chords on her old mandolin with its two bass guitar strings, write song after song, and sleep five and six in a bed with her brothers and sisters.

But there was something more than melody in Dolly's soul. There exists in the mountain chains of the Appalachians and the Great Smokies a centuries-old bardic tradition from the British Isles, passed down from generation to generation through song, story, and "play-party" games, which gives the simple country speech of the isolated people a lyrical overlay. Dolly's song lyrics exhibit this oral poetic tradition; they are rich in simile and metaphor, always evocative of real life; they are pictures painted with words.

All Dolly's songs were autobiographical; they dealt with the themes she knew best: growing up barefoot; a passel of brothers and sisters; the strength and pride of her parents; her deep religious feelings and faith in Jesus; the death of a child or of a beloved relative or friend in the Korean War; the love between mother and babies; the respect she had for her father and her grandfather—meaningful subjects that expressed true and recognizable emotions. To strike a chord in the heart of the listener, a song must be pulled from the very heart of the writer and singer.

When Dolly Parton was eight years old, on a momentous and joyful day, her mother's brother, Uncle Robert Owens, who believed in Dolly from the start, gave her a real guitar of her own, a little Martin. It was then, for the first time, that she learned to play full chords on a complete set of strings. It was to be the first definite step up on Dolly's stairway to the stars. Once she had her Martin, her "real" guitar, nothing could stop her.

Her childhood fantasies of fame and fortune took on an even straighter direction: 200 miles west, to Nashville, the Mecca of country music, and, especially, the "Grand Ole Opry." Until you had been invited to sing on the "Opry," you weren't anybody to be reckoned with. But once you had, you could be on your way to being a star, to a recording contract on a country and western label and to concert appearances and road shows. And who knew? One might get even luckier, and be awarded that prize valued above all others—to be chosen as an "Opry" regular. Dolly knew that there was a place called Nashville, where she could go to become a star. But it seemed to her to be a million miles away. Even so, day by day, Nashville increasingly became the bright, beckoning focus of little Dolly Parton's driving ambitions.

# Chapter Two

## Singing for Money

I always knew I was somebody.
I dreamed big dreams and I got
out early.

—Dolly Parton

But even the most talented and precocious child
doesn't run until she learns to walk, and Nashville wasn't just sitting there waiting for Dolly
Rebecca Parton, amateur, no matter how gifted
her friends and family believed she was. So Dolly
began singing in public.

She was already singing in church on Sun-
days, so it seemed almost natural that she would
sing in school on Mondays. Not her own songs,
though, but hymns, a kind of continuation of the

Church of God, because the one-room school-house in Mountain View held chapel services every Monday morning. Either they had never heard of the Constitutional separation of Church and State, or they didn't much care, and what federal agency was going to come down salty on a little backwoods schoolhouse with not more than 15 students in all the grades put together?

Singing hymns in public led Dolly to singing old folk songs and ballads, as Dolly's confidence in herself and her powers grew. It was still a tiny world that surrounded her—family, church, and school probably didn't come to 100 different people all told—but Dolly's philosophy was always, "You gotta start somewhere, even if it's small. Anything's better than sitting still." So she sang for that 100, and dreamed of singing for thousands, even millions.

Good attendance at school wasn't easy for the mountain children of east Tennessee in the 1950s. In Dolly's day there weren't paved roads or scheduled school buses painted bright yellow. Boys and girls had to walk miles to school, some of the way over rocky and treacherous back roads, which never got plowed out in the winter.

"There weren't many people who lived way back in the holler where we did. We walked a long, long way to school. It was only a one-room schoolhouse that had no more than 10 or 15 kids in the whole school and one teacher. We sat in rows by grades. Maybe there was one or two kids in the first grade, might be two or three in the second, one in the third, and so on. Teacher'd sit with us grades one at a time, while the other grades read

31

their books or did their exercises in their notebooks till she could get to them."

Sometimes Dolly would arrive at the little schoolhouse with freezing feet; warm boots were a rich kid's luxury. She'd have to thaw out her blue feet in front of the wood-burning stove before she could begin her studies.

Often, too, the children of farmer folk would have to miss days, even weeks, of school when the crops had to be seeded, or dug out and stored. Survival took priority over education. "In the mountains, schoolin' is just not that important," recalls Dolly. "My daddy didn't 'specially want me to go to school, and my mama, she didn't care."

Nevertheless, Dolly was determined to get an education and be the first Parton youngster to graduate from high school. Even though she was more motivated by music than by arithmetic and spelling, she was bright enough to make up the schoolwork she missed on her absentee days.

It was around this same time that the Partons moved once again, to a farm in Caton's Chapel, about 40 or 50 acres, and there they would remain until Dolly graduated from high school in 1964. Caton's Chapel wasn't even a dot on the map of Tennessee; it was little more than a name and a cluster of cabins not far from the church.

When Dolly was eight, she attended a music show at the Pines Theater in Sevierville with her mother and some of her brothers and sisters. It took all the courage the small girl had to ask the man in charge if she could go up on the stage and sing, but Dolly was never short on courage. The audience loved her, and it was her first real taste of applause. She had sung before on a TV show in Knoxville, but that had been with her class from school; this was just Dolly alone. If she needed any extra assurance that singing in front of an audience was what she was born to do, the sound of clapping and cheering gave her that reinforcement.

Like many mountain families whose cabins had no electricity, the Partons owned a battery radio, which, Dolly said, "would whistle in and out. I remember us pourin' water on that ground wire to try an' pick up 'The Lone Ranger.' " Not that the family could always afford new batteries, but whenever the batteries were working, they listened to "Grand Ole Opry."

More than just a radio program, "Grand Ole Opry" is a Saturday night institution all over the Southland. It had started out over radio station WSM as a program called "WSM Barn Dance" on November 28, 1925, and it hasn't missed a performance since, the longest-running continuous radio program in America. Its combination of earthy, hee-haw hillbilly humor and the best singers and songs in country and western music had made the "Opry" so popular that by the time Dolly was born, hundreds of people would get up extra early every Saturday morning just to line up outside the broadcast studio at the old Ryman Auditorium in the heart of downtown Nashville, hoping to get a precious ticket to see the stars in person.

And big stars they were—the biggest. At first, the "Opry" featured mostly fiddlers and banjos in bands, the Fruit Jar Drinkers, Dr. Humphrey

Bate and the Possum Hunters, the Gully Jumpers, and other bands like them. But soon, individual stars would begin to emerge, and by the time the Parton family was crowded around the old battery portable, country music legends were appearing on the "Opry."

There were hillbilly comics like beloved Sara Ophelia Colley, known as Minnie Pearl, with her funny hats and her trademark "How-dee!"; the team of Lonzo and Oscar; Jerry Clower; singers and songwriters such as the immortal Hank Williams and his sad songs; the King of Country Music, Roy Acuff, and his band, the Smoky Mountain Boys; Maybelle Carter and her daughters; Bill Monroe; Ernest Tubb and his steel guitar; Red Foley; Chet Atkins; Eddy Arnold; Hank Snow; a very young Johnny Cash; Patsy Cline; Jean Shepard; Kitty Wells—the list goes on and on. These were the important men and women who had influenced the very way country music was expected to sound. Most of them were songwriters as well as performers.

Back then, tickets to the "Grand Ole Opry" didn't cost big bucks, but times have changed. Today, the "Opry" is on television as well as radio, it broadcasts from its own new concrete-steel-and-glass 4,400-seat Opry House, and a good seat costs $10. Nashville has become "Music City, U.S.A.," with its other attractions, the Country Music Hall of Fame, and its theme park, Opryland. On a good weekend, perhaps 20,000 tourists will pass through Nashville, buying tickets and snapping their flashbulbs.

But the biggest attraction is "Grand Ole Opry";

the show is still the same magnet drawing aspiring country singers as it was when Dolly was a girl. The "Opry" is the country equivalent of an actor's goal of Broadway or Hollywood, or the old vaudevillian's dream of playing the palace; it's the big time, now as then.

The first genius behind the "Opry" was founder, manager, announcer, and master of ceremonies Judge George D. Hay, a father figure to his many performers. In his later years, he set down in writing the philosophy of the "Grand Ole Opry," a formula still adhered to. Reading his words, one comes to understand what made the program so very successful for so very long.

"Our show is presented for the rural and industrial workers throughout the states. Above all, we try to keep it 'homey.' Home folks do the work of the world; they win the wars and raise the families. Many of our geniuses come from simple folk who adhere to the fundamental principles of honesty included in the Ten Commandments. The 'Grand Ole Opry' expresses those qualities which come from these good people."

Although Judge Hay wasn't aware of it when he wrote those words, he was describing Dolly Parton's genius to a "T."

But if the "Opry" is the biggest country music show on the air, it's not by any means the only one. When Dolly was growing up, there were famous radio programs such as "Louisiana Hayride" out of Shreveport, "Big D Jamboree" from— where else?— Dallas, "National Barn Dance," broadcast from Chicago, and many others. Just about every city in the South has its own mini-version of a big-time country music show, heard locally and featuring local talent. Patsy Cline got her start on a local show, "Jimmy Dean's Town and Country Jamboree." So did many others; it would be wrong to underestimate the value of these 5,000-watt "Hoedowns" and "Hayrides" in giving some of the superstars of today that first, vital push that would get their careers into gear.

The only radio station of any importance close to Sevierville was WIVK in Knoxville, Tennessee, about 40 miles away. Thanks to WIVK and a very energetic man named Cas Walker, little Dolly Parton would receive a push early in life.

Cas Walker was by all accounts a dynamo; he was just about everywhere one looked in Knoxville, running a successful chain of supermarkets or running for mayor or a seat on the town council—it was all the same to him. Politics and business had made him something of a local celebrity; he was not only elected three times mayor of Knoxville, but was the only mayor in the city's history to be recalled in a special election and kicked out of office.

Where Cas really shone was in his first love, country music. Not only did he pick a little and sing a little himself, but he sponsored country music programs on radio and TV, in addition to live performances in theaters. Those who knew him then say Walker was a colorful personality, and he would be of major importance in furthering Dolly's career. He would be her first talent scout, and the first impresario to pay her to sing.

It was Cas Walker who had brought that country music show to the Pines Theater in Sevierville,

Cas Walker who had sponsored the TV program on which Dolly's class had appeared. His most important and successful contribution to the furtherance of country music was an early-morning TV show, "The Farm and Home Hour," broadcast over WIVK every morning at 5:30, with a kind of reprise live radio show around noon, and another TV program in the evening. It was the most natural thing in the world for eight-year-old Dolly to go and sing on Cas Walker's shows.

Forty miles is a long way for a little girl to travel to sing at 5:30 in the morning; to do so, she had to get up at 4 A.M. But Dolly was no ordinary little girl. Her uncle, Bill Owens, himself an ambitious musician and a staunch supporter of Dolly's, the man who gave Dolly her little Martin guitar, would drive her down from Sevierville, and drive her back in time for school.

"I heard her singin' many times," says Uncle Bill, describing Dolly's first real audition for Cas. "And, man, even then she was mighty good. She sang when she was washin' the dishes, or puttin' the little ones to bed. The thought came to me that she oughta be singin' on Cas Walker's programs, so I drove her on down there. This particular show was comin' from a downstairs studio. When Dolly started singin,' why, announcers from upstairs and the other people from all over the building came in to listen to her. She made a big hit, and Cas Walker hired her on the spot."

Dolly sang on the Walker radio shows from time to time from the age of eight to the age of ten. Then she took another step up on the ladder of success.

Cas Walker asked Dolly Parton to be a regular on his show, and he offered her a salary of $20 a week! To a ten-year-old, it was a fortune. And in 1956, it was no small amount.

Nineteen fifty-six was the epicenter of the Eisenhower years. America was in the grip of atomic fever; people building and stocking bomb shelters in their backyards, determined to be dug in safely when the Russian atom bomb exploded over Topeka. But, even with the Cold War, the Hungarian uprising, Sputnik, the Berlin Wall, and all the truly terrifying global events, America was enjoying a postwar boom time, plus all the technological miracles that Americans had been promised and had been waiting for all during the long grim war. Americans went on a buying spree, and, with wartime price controls lifted, costs kept rising and inflation set in.

Music was changing, too, moving away from the bland and saccharine melodies of crew-cut harmonic groups toward bouncier singers like Peggy Lee and Doris Day, toward rhythm and blues and toward something new called rock 'n' roll. Nineteen fifty-six was the year of Elvis Presley, of "Love Me Tender," "Hound Dog," and "Heartbreak Hotel." Among ten-year-old Dolly's personal favorite singers were Brenda Lee and Connie Francis.

In 1956, a country music songwriter, Ivory Joe Hunter, had two hits that each sold over 1,000,000 records, "My Wish Came True," and "I Need You So," which Elvis, Pat Boone, and Sonny James recorded. And a twenty-four-year-old singer named Johnny Cash was creating a sensation on

"Grand Ole Opry" with a song called "I Walk the Line." For the first time, urban America was becoming aware of Nashville, Tennessee.

So there was Dolly Parton at the tender age of ten, singing on the radio just like a professional. She worked hard for that $20; Cas Walker got his money's worth and more. When school was in session, her appearances were, naturally, scheduled around her classroom attendance, but she usually managed the early show, and sometimes even the midday one. On weekends and school holidays, she did every broadcast; and on Wednesday nights, when Cas Walker had a live TV show, she would stay late and sing on that, too. When her Uncle Bill didn't drive her back and forth, her Aunt Estelle Watson, who lived in Knoxville, did. Her family had a powerful faith in Dolly, whose energy and persistence impressed them as much as her talent.

During the summer months, Dolly stayed on in Knoxville with her Aunt Estelle and sang on Cas Walker's shows three times a day, three days a week. Once, when she was away in Knoxville, her precious Martin guitar was loaned out, and the borrower was careless. "That hurt me real bad," Dolly said. "It had its side busted out and the neck got broke off. I reckon some kids had jumped up and down on it or somethin', never did find out what had happened. So I put it away and said that when I got enough money together, first thing I'd do I'd get my git-tar fixed. Took me a while, though.

"They said they'd pay me twenty dollars a week to start with. My aunt in Knoxville said she would take me up to the radio stations and the TV shows if Mama and Daddy would let me stay, and she did. And I sang country music, some songs I wrote. I was singin' by myself and playin' the guitar. But I guess it was because I was a little kid they were sayin' that the audience liked it, because I wasn't really that good."

If she wasn't "that good," she was getting better fast. Music was now the central obsession of Dolly's life. Not only was she singing on the radio and on TV, she was making a round of local personal appearances in church halls, school auditoriums, Kiwanis clubs, and anywhere a country music show was performed. And she was cutting tapes, at night, in the studios at WIVK.

Dolly and her uncles Bill and Louis Owens would drive down from Sevierville to record demonstration tapes of the songs they had written to send to Nashville. The studio engineers donated their time, the studio musicians would back up their arrangements, and Dolly's sisters would sing the harmony. The main targets of all this energy and labor were the Nashville music publishers, record companies, and, of course, "Grand Ole Opry." "I never stopped writin' songs or sendin' off tapes," Dolly remembers.

When Dolly was thirteen, she actually made it on the "Opry," although her appearance on the show was strictly a fluke. For one thing, the "Opry" was a union shop, which meant that no performer not in the musicians' union could play the show. When they told Dolly she had to be "in the union," she had no idea what the word meant.

"I kind of had the idea that it might be a costume, or maybe a room to practice in," says Dolly.

For another thing, the "Opry" had a rule that nobody under the age of eighteen could play the show. Even though Dolly's burgeoning and abundant figure could easily be mistaken for an eighteen-year-old's, she was five years under age. It was faith and determination alone, plus persistent nagging, that finally got her on the program.

But none of that was in Dolly's mind when she made the trip. Her Uncle Bill borrowed a car, and the two of them drove to Nashville; their goal, to get Dolly on the stage of the Ryman Auditorium and let the world hear her sing.

"First time I was on the 'Opry,' I went with the intentions of bein' on. Nobody ever told me that you couldn't do anything you wanted to do. I just always thought, *Well, all you gotta do is just go there, and if you sing good enough, you can be on the 'Grand Ole Opry.'* Gettin' up the nerve was the hardest part, but we were already blessed with more nerve than sense anyway."

Once backstage at the "Opry," Bill and Dolly buttonholed everybody about getting Dolly onstage to sing. At first they had no luck at all. Dolly was too young, they said, and besides, her name wasn't on the list. But Dolly persisted; she wasn't one to give up easily, especially after coming 200 miles.

Finally, she got a break. She had approached a country music star named Jimmy C. Newman, who was scheduled to go on next, imploring him to help her. The way things went on the "Opry" was that every performer came on and did two numbers back to back. So impressed was he by her determination and her pretty face that he gave up one of his own spots on the show, turning it over to Dolly. He told Johnny Cash to announce Dolly Parton's name before his.

Suddenly, a long-held dream came true. All at once, Dolly found herself in front of a microphone and a huge, dedicated country music audience on the most important show of them all. She sang a George Jones song, "If You Want to Be My Baby," and "just tore the house down. I had to sing it over and over and over. I thought I was a star. That was the first time for me."

Maybe Dolly didn't suspect it then, and maybe she did, but it would be the first of many times that Dolly would be tearing the house down on the "Opry."

After that, Dolly and Bill would from time to time drive the 200 miles back and forth to the song publishers, record companies, and concert promoters of Music City, making the rounds, knocking on doors, looking for the big breakthrough, with no success.

"My Uncle Bill had him an old car with the sides all busted in," Dolly told her biographer, Alanna Nash. "We'd save up enough money to go back and forth to Nashville, tryin' to get somethin' goin' for us. Uncle Bill said I was goin' to be a star, and I was fool enough to believe him. So we'd take out every time we'd get a chance. We'd sleep in the car and clean up in fillin' stations."

In 1959, when Dolly was thirteen, her Uncle Robert was in the service, stationed in Lake Charles, Louisiana. Lake Charles is the home of Goldband Records, a small studio that recorded a number of major country and western artists at the beginning of their careers while they were still unknowns, including Freddy Fender, Mickey Gilley, and Larry Williams. Dolly packed up her repaired Martin, got on a bus, and went down to Lake Charles to cut her first record.

For Goldband she recorded two sides: One was a lively teen number called "Puppy Love," which she wrote herself and which she sang in Brenda Lee style; the other, a sad song about a girl gone astray, "Girl Left Alone," she had written with her Uncle Bill Owens. Not quite five feet tall, Dolly was so short that she had to sit on a high stool to reach the microphone. The record was released and went nowhere, but it was one more piece of valuable experience for Dolly's growing collection.

By the time she was thirteen years old, Dolly had reached her full growth—in more ways than one. Having attained her full height of 5 feet, she continued growing in other directions. Her hips grew round, full, and womanly, and that amazing bosom, Dolly's most outstanding physical attribute, had reached its full size. No more little-girl calico dresses for Dolly Parton. Always concerned with her appearance, she graduated to skintight clothes.

She bought her jeans small, and shrunk them down even smaller, until they hugged her little round behind so tightly she could barely sit down. She teased her hair into the latest styles, experimenting with hair coloring to lighten it, and with other cosmetic products to give it body. But its appearance never quite met with her approval.

*Leonore Fleischer*

Thanks to her appearances on television, Dolly had already become proficient in the art of makeup, and now she wore it almost every day, layering it on thickly. At this time she began to experiment with wigs, covering her own shoulder-length, very fine brown hair with masses of artificial golden curls. The Dolly Parton image was beginning to emerge, like the butterflies she loves, and with which she so identifies that she has chosen them as her personal symbol.

Now she became popular with boys, but for the wrong reasons, as she herself has recalled a little sadly.

"When I was thirteen I looked like I was twenty-five. A lotta stories went around about me, but they was a lotta lies. It was because I had these big boobs and this big behind, and this little tiny waist. I got to lookin' real mature, and from then on I tried to make the most of my looks and to improve them, and that meant I wore my clothes tight, and I mean *skintight!* I wore makeup and flirted a lot with boys. Sometimes I was embarrassed by my figure, but mostly I accepted what God gave me. I was popular in high school, but not in the right way. But I reckon it didn't bother me a lot, 'cause music was on my mind a lot more than boys." Even so, Dolly found time to flirt and tell dirty jokes, aware that some of the other students were snickering about her behind her back. Some were even convinced that she'd filled her bras with tissue in order to give the *appearance* of a big chest. But if the hair and eyelashes were false, at least her chest was quite real, a gift from Mother Nature.

"A lot of people take me wrong," she told reporter Jerry Bailey, "because I look like the type of person that might be tryin' to show off, because I wear gaudy clothes. I guess it's because when I was little I never really had anythin' at all, and when I would see somebody dressed up real fancy, that would just impress me no end. I just thought that one of these days I was going' to wear fancy clothes and hairdos and makeup and shiny jewelry. It's just part of my personality."

At fourteen, Dolly entered high school, a different kind of world from the one-room schoolhouse and the supportive comfort of family and friends. Sevier County High School was a much wider arena than Dolly had grown up accustomed to; boys and girls from the small city of Sevierville mingled somewhat uncomfortably with kids from the mountains. But even among the country kids Dolly Parton stood out like a bandaged thumb.

High school is a crucial passage in life. Even as boys and girls take those first tentative steps on their way to independence, trying to find out who they are and of what they are capable, conformity is prized. And remember that we are in the year 1960, before "doing your own thing" became the thing to conform to.

At fourteen, Dolly, with her woman's figure and the gaudiness of her appearance, was very different from the ponytailed bobby-soxers in poodle skirts. Boys would snicker with embarrassed delight and girls would sniff indignantly at the sight of those majestic breasts that defied concealment. Dolly found herself with virtually no friends, although she did have a claque of fans among the teen-agers who were mountain kids like herself, and who followed her appearances on local radio and TV. The city kids weren't impressed.

Another thing that caused a rift between Dolly Parton and her schoolmates was her certainty that she would someday be a star. Hadn't she already cut a record? Hadn't she appeared on the "Grand Ole Opry"? Wasn't she still singing on Cas Walker's TV and radio shows? By the time she graduated from Sevier County High, her salary would be $60 a week. She was a professional entertainer; the others were just high school kids. She couldn't get excited about the teen-aged dating and the kind of clothes that turned them on; they couldn't share her dreams and ambitions. Also, to the more citified boys and girls, she was the worst kind of hick, the professional hillbilly who was making money at it. And, though they would rather have died than admit it, they must have been a little jealous of her.

Even though she persevered, determined to become the first Parton to earn a high school diploma, Dolly hated school. The confinement of it, its rigid schedule, stifled that butterfly soul of hers that yearned to fly free. Besides the promise of a diploma, the main thing that kept Dolly inside school walls was the fact that things were worse at home than they were at school. Her mother was always ill, and there was the constant squabbling among the Parton siblings, and the wailing of babies cutting teeth.

Intelligent though she was, Dolly wasn't a good student, and the main thing that got her by was her grade in "band," 98. The 98 pulled up the rest of her average. She also did well in home economics, thanks to good teaching at home, and she became a member of the Future Homemakers of America, which was something like the female equivalent of the Junior Chamber of Commerce.

Even though she chafed under the discipline of high school, while other students laughed at her behind her back, Dolly shrugged and pretended not to care. Music was the center of her life. During the years when girls are pursuing boys and boys are pursuing their daddies' cars, Dolly was pursuing her career.

As for her outrageous appearance, Dolly just smiles when asked about it. "I like to be gaudy. It makes me different. When I first started singin', I decided I would dress in gaudy, outrageous clothes because it fit my outgoin' personality. It was also like a dream come true. I always wanted to be glittery and stand out. Why should I hide the parts of me that are extreme? I just try to make the extreme more extreme. Life, you know, can be kinda borin', so I like to spice things up a little."

It wasn't until she began playing snare drums in the high school marching band that Dolly made a few friends and became more popular. The band was important to her, and still is. After she achieved stardom, Dolly played a number of benefit concerts in Sevierville, turning over the proceeds to the Sevier County High School band to buy equipment, instruments, and uniforms. She also established a scholarship fund at the school in 1970. Now the same boys and girls who didn't talk to her in the old high school days are the men and women who proclaim Dolly Parton Day in Sevierville.

When she was fourteen years old, Tree International Publishing of Nashville signed her to a songwriter's contract, and at the age of fifteen she cut her second single, "It May Not Kill Me but It's Sure Gonna Hurt," released on the Mercury label. It was a song she and her Uncle Bill wrote, "but it never did nothin'," as Dolly told Toby Thompson in his *Village Voice* interview more than fifteen years later. "I came back home after that, decidin' I wasn't gonna do nothin' else till after I graduated."

The fact that she did in fact graduate from high school is amazing when one considers that she spent more time writing songs than term papers, and more time singing than learning. But graduate she did, the first in the Parton family to earn a high school diploma, " 'cause I wanted to say I did it."

She was graduated on a Friday in June 1964. As part of the ceremony, there was a baccalaureate at the First Baptist Church in Sevierville, when each graduating senior stood up and announced what goal he or she was going to work toward.

Dolly didn't falter when her turn came around. She told the audience what she had always told everybody who would listen—she was going to Nashville to become a singer and a songwriter. Only this time it wasn't only a dream. The bus fare was in her purse, and when a ripple of derisive laughter passed through the audience, Dolly just lifted her stubborn little round chin and her eyes threw out sparks. She knew better.

Later, she drove over to WIVK for her last appearance on local TV, and announced on the air that she was "goin' to Nashville to be a country music singer and songwriter, and I ain't comin' back until I make it!"

Early the next morning, Saturday, an eighteen-year-old Dolly Parton, dressed in a modest brown dress with long sleeves and a high collar, her hair in a bouffant flip, was on a Greyhound bus heading for Nashville. She took with her a cheap cardboard suitcase, tied up with string so it wouldn't burst open, and crammed with just about everything she owned in the world. She also carried along her Martin guitar, a folder full of songs she wrote herself, the love and the fears of her anxious parents, and her dirty laundry. She had left town in such a hurry that she hadn't had time to wash her clothes.

But Dolly Rebecca Parton didn't care; she was anxious to get started on fulfilling her destiny. Laundry could wait; Nashville couldn't.

# Chapter Three

## Nashville and Carl

I never had a doubt I would
make it, because refusing to think
I *couldn't* make it is the reason
I *could*.

—Dolly Parton

Believe it or not, that sack of dirty laundry was
to turn out to be a godsend; it would be the cause
of yet another major change in Dolly's life. But
let's back up a little.

Every year, high school graduates from small
towns, villages, and hamlets all over America
come to the big city with stars in their eyes and
no money in their pockets. Whether they land in
New York or Los Angeles or Nashville makes no

difference—it's all the same. The same ambitions, the same dreams, the same new feeling of freedom and independence, the same sweet taste of being on one's own at last. The same fears and doubts, the same struggles, the same longing for friends and family back home. They work, they go hungry, they meet rejection, their hearts break again and again; they see their bright dreams first tarnish, then fade. Most of those kids go back home again and marry the girl or boy next door, go into daddy's hardware business, or raise a couple of kids. One in perhaps 10,000 becomes a star.

But that one person in 10,000 has what it takes, and it takes a lot more than talent alone. It takes determination to make it no matter what life throws at you—aching feet or an aching, hungry belly or an aching heart. It takes the ability to roll with the punches, to face rejection by looking it straight on and saying, "Whatever you may say, I *know* I'm good, and I'm going to *prove it*." It takes what Dolly Parton was born with.

A few weeks before Dolly graduated from Sevier County High, her Uncle Bill had moved to Nashville with his wife, Cathy, and baby son, and had rented a place with room in it for Dolly. Bill was playing in his own band, backing up Carl and Pearl Butler, and he was out of town a lot, and Cathy was holding down a job as a waitress, so they really needed Dolly as a live-in baby-sitter for her baby cousin. Besides, Bill and Dolly were a singing-and-songwriting team, and her uncle was certain that Dolly and he were going to open the doors to success as a team. It was only because Dolly was going to be staying with near kinfolk that her parents reluctantly allowed her to leave home, especially to go to the big city.

"I felt that Dolly was too young to be turned loose alone in a city the size of Nashville," said her mother.

But Dolly saw Nashville as her only possible future, and her Uncle Bill, who was ambitious for himself as well as for her, agreed. Bill had made contacts in the music world, and he had confidence in his own talents and Dolly's. Whether they would make it as singers or songwriters was as yet unknown, but make it they would, of that they were equally certain. Besides, even Dolly had a slim contact in Music City; she was still under contract to Tree Publishing, even if the Mercury record they had arranged for her hadn't been a hit or anything like a hit.

This was the summer of 1964, and the times they were a-changing. A President of the United States had been brutally assassinated, shocking the world and traumatizing a generation. Lyndon Johnson was in the White House, touring Appalachia and declaring war on poverty, while an undeclared war was beginning to escalate in a faraway place called Vietnam. More than 100 American lives had been lost to date. A group of Liverpool moptops called the Beatles were revolutionizing music, and other groups like the Rolling Stones were imitating them with almost as much success. This was also to be, although nobody knew it, a civil rights summer, when the bodies of three missing civil rights workers would be dug up from a shallow grave in Mississippi. The South would be a-changing, too.

But Dolly's head was filled with lyrics and melodies, not global and political changes. She was eighteen years old, and all filled out—more than all filled out. Men's heads turned when this tiny pretty thing with the sparkling smile, the tiny waist, and the big boobs came sashaying down the street. She had stars in her eyes and a suitcase bursting with her songs. Dolly Parton was in Nashville at last, ready and eager to begin a new life. Stardom, here she came!

With the rise of "Grand Ole Opry" to predominance in country music, the heart of the business became Nashville. Not only did many of the star performers on the show buy or build luxurious homes and ranches in and around the city, but management, record companies, music publishers, studio personnel, sidemen, backup singers, show promoters, and just about everyone else connected with the business had moved there, making it "Music City, U.S.A." The streets around the Ryman Auditorium were choked with bars, honky-tonks, and cheap hotels. Some of them, like Tootsie's Orchid Lounge, were favorite after-work watering holes of the country music greats; others did a thriving business in the overflow of the not-so-great. Downtown Nashville possessed a sleazy, neon-bright ambience that was alien to everything Dolly Parton knew growing up. Even so, she fell in love with the city on sight, declaring "I'm home."

Remember that sack of dirty laundry? The first thing Dolly had to do when she arrived on the Owenses' doorstep in South Nashville was get that dirty laundry clean so she would have something to wear. Off she went to the Wishy-Washy Laundromat near her uncle's home. The owners ought to put up a bronze plaque there—if, in fact, the laundromat is still in business—to commemorate the fact that, on the first day she was in Nashville, within hours of her arrival Dolly Rebecca Parton met the man who was to be her future husband.

Dolly put her clothes into the machine, dropped in the coins, and started the wash cycle. But she was never a girl to sit still and wait. Outside, Nashville was beckoning; it was a bright day in early summer, and she was in a strange town. So she bought a Royal Crown Cola from the dispenser and, bottle in hand, went out to have a look at the town, or at least that part of Nashville that was close to the laundromat. What she was doing was walking around the block, sipping her soda, and enjoying the sight of new places.

"We met at the Wishy-Washy, and it's been wishy-washy ever since," joked Dolly for the thousandth time, on the "Oprah Winfrey Show" in April 1987, when she and Carl Dean had been married for 21 years. For theirs has been an enduring marriage. You can call it unique, since they are rarely in the same house at the same time, but their relationship began in the most traditional way—boy sees girl, boy picks up girl, girl marries boy.

On that fateful day in June 1964, Carl Dean was at the impressionable age of twenty-one, and how his eyes must have popped out of his head at the sight of those dimples, those round, rosy cheeks, and bright eyes, not to mention those ... other attributes of Dolly's sensational figure. More than likely, Carl wasn't even thinking about the possibility of a brain under that fluffy yellow hair (by now Dolly had dyed her brown hair a whitish-blond, but she still had it covered with wigs; in those days the wigs were beehives and Jackie Kennedy bouffants), so it must have come as a pleasant surprise to discover that this pretty girl from the country could think, too.

A native of Nashville and an asphalt paving contractor, Carl Dean was about to go into the army, and was enjoying the time he had left by "cruising." Although today the word carries a heavy sexual overtone, in 1964 it was a relatively innocent pastime. Boys would drive around in their cars looking for pretty girls, and try to persuade them to go for a ride. Naturally, they hoped they'd get lucky, but most of the time it turned out to be nothing more than an afternoon's or evening's flirtation, with maybe a hamburger and a soda thrown in.

When Carl saw Dolly, he did what any red-blooded American boy would do—he leaned on his horn to get her attention and waved at her like crazy. Dolly, naïve and country-friendly, waved back.

"I got me a big RC Cola," recalls Dolly, "and when my clothes were washin' in the laundromat, I went out walkin' to see what I could see of Nashville. I was jes' walkin' down the street and along came this really handsome boy in a white Chevrolet. An' he was flirtin' with me. In the country, you speak to everybody, and me bein' from the country, I didn't want him to think I was stuck-up or nothin', so I waved back. Didn't mean nothin' special by it; I was just bein' friendly. Well, maybe in the back of my mind somewhere I was noticin' how cute and handsome he was, but mostly I was just bein' friendly."

The next thing either of them knew, he'd pulled his late-model white Chevy over to the curb and got out to walk alongside Dolly. Soon, they were deep in conversation. He asked her where she was from, and Dolly, certain that he would never know where Sevierville was, told him she was from Knoxville.

Explaining that her clothes were at this minute spinning in a machine at the Wishy-Washy, and that she was just taking a little stroll to see some of Nashville before the rinse cycle was over, Dolly flashed her dimples, and Carl Dean was lost.

Naturally, Carl wanted to take Dolly riding in his car and show her all the Nashville sights. Just as naturally, Dolly was tempted by this tall, good-looking young man (Carl is her favorite type—tall and thin and dark-haired, the perfect contrast to her little fluffy blond self), but her mama had raised her right. One did not go riding with strangers, no matter how cute, so Dolly said a definite "no." Carl got out of the car and walked her back to the Wishy-Washy, the two of them talking away, especially Dolly. Even on her first day in Nashville, Dolly was homesick for her mountains and her family, and she found this handsome stranger easy to talk to.

Up until then, Dolly hadn't dated much. It wasn't that boys didn't want to take her out—how could they help wanting to, with that face and that figure and that merry disposition and giggly laugh? It wasn't that Dolly didn't want to; she was perfectly normal, with natural development and urges. But Dolly had always been too busy with her music to pay much attention to boys. She didn't have weekends or school holidays free, and she would often have to break a date with a boy because she had been hired to sing somewhere.

But Carl was different from the high school boys and the band members or studio musicians she knew and with whom she occasionally went out. There was a mature, quiet strength about him that must have reminded Dolly of Robert Lee Parton. Very often, girls who have grown up with strong fathers choose strong men as husbands; they have come to rely upon and need that masculine strength. More importantly, they recognize that strength when they encounter it.

There was something else about Carl that kindled a spark in Dolly. Whenever she told boys about her dreams of stardom, of making it to the top as a country music star, it had somehow turned them off. Sometimes it would make them laugh, but usually the thought of Dolly Parton as tomorrow's star provoked resentment. Masculine and feminine roles were rigidly defined in those days, and it was the man who brought home the bacon, the woman who cooked it up in the pan, served it, then washed the dishes, swept the kitchen, and put the babies to bed. Anything about a girl's hopes and plans for a career was very threatening to a boy.

Of course, Dolly had gone out with some band musicians by the time she was eighteen—pickers and singers from the radio station and guys she had met on her gigs. They were more understanding of Dolly's ambitions for a career in music, but there was a jealous tinge in that understanding, as though she were a rival for the one and only opening for stardom. Or maybe it was her obvious talent they resented.

Carl was different from all of them. When Dolly told him, as she did, right away, about her ambitions and about the suitcase crammed with songs, he was instantly supportive. There wasn't a jealous bone in his body, and he didn't feel threatened by the thought of Dolly's career. He responded to Dolly's self-assurance. Because of his maturity and his own self-assurance as a man and as a person, he took her exactly as she was—songs, guitar, ambitions, and all. Although Dolly wasn't aware of it at the time, this was exactly what she had been looking for in a guy of her own.

Perhaps the most important quality about Carl was that he wasn't a part of the music business. He had his own life to live, his own living to pursue—his father owned an asphalt-paving business—and music was a field that Dolly could have all to herself. Which is the way she always liked it.

So there they were, side by side at the Wishy-Washy, stuffing Dolly's laundry into the dryer and getting acquainted. By now Carl was really interested in this bright-eyed hillbilly girl with the big dreams, and he could see that he had made an impression on her, too. He continued to press her to go out with him, and Dolly continued to evade him, even though saying no went against her innermost wishes. But she really didn't know this boy at all, and her mother and father would be horrified and furious if they knew she had let a strange boy pick her up on the street so easily.

In the end, Carl Dean went back to his Chevy, but not before he had made a date with Dolly to call on her the next day at her uncle's house, the only right and proper way for a mountain girl to begin seeing a boy.

And that's how the love story of Dolly and Carl began. He came over to the apartment the following day, about two in the afternoon, and "We sat on the steps. Actually, it was the fire escape. The next day he came back, and the next day he came back, until I got to know him pretty well. When my aunt, who was working at Shoney's, got her first day off, we had our first date. We talked for about five days before I went out with him."

Carl would come and visit her at Uncle Bill's South Nashville apartment, but she'd never let him inside the door, because Bill was playing gigs and Cathy was away working. Instead, the two of them would sit on the fire escape, hold hands, and talk about their "somedays." And if a kiss or two was exchanged, well, surely it was nobody's business but theirs.

On their first real date, Carl took her home to meet his parents, and that made it official. They were going together. Dolly was ecstatic, and her letters home were filled with *Carl this* and *Carl that* and *Carl says* and *Carl does*.

But even falling in love with Carl didn't stand in the way of Dolly's ambitions. She had come to Nashville to be a star, and she began to work at it as soon as she unpacked her suitcases.

A letter she wrote home very soon after she left Sevier County is filled with a girlish blend of enthusiastic optimism, love, nostalgia, loneliness, and the thrill of independence. She called herself "a little lonesome and a whole lot homesick," but assured her mama and daddy that she had arrived safely and was settling into her new, strange life. Dolly was afraid they would be worrying themselves sick over her back home, and, while things were still striking her as very different from the mountains, she was getting used to the new ways, and had no intention of going back.

Dolly hadn't realized quite how much she loved her parents "and all them noisy kids" until she had cut the cord and broken away. There had been tears shed at the parting, shed on both sides, and Dolly had continued to cry almost all the way to Nashville. More than once, she had wanted to turn around and go back. But her dream lay ahead of her, not behind.

Everybody who knew Dolly knew how badly she had always wanted to go to Nashville and be a singer and songwriter. Dolly had great faith in herself. She knew that if she tried long enough and hard enough, and let nothing discourage her—no amount of rejection, no amount of sheer hard work—she would succeed at last. "Someday I'll make it," was always in her thoughts.

Meanwhile, although she was always short of money, she kept up a brave front, assuring her parents that everything was fine and that she did not need any cash, because she had landed a job singing on an early-morning television program, *The Eddie Hill Show*. She also had a few nibbles from other performers, who might record a couple of her songs. Dolly assured her parents that she was not going hungry, when in truth, often she was; she was always broke. And, knowing what worried them nearly as much as her starving to death, she did renew her promises to be a good girl and not to get into trouble or yield to the temptations of the big city.

But it was a long way from a singing gig on a local television program to real success. Dolly and Bill kept making the rounds of Music Row, knocking on doors that never seemed to open to them. On Music Row were the offices of the major producers and promoters, and such publishing companies as Window Music, Mercury Studios, Combine Music, MGM Records, and Columbia and Capitol Records.

Naturally, Dolly wrote an autobiographical song

about those lean and hungry, frustrating Nashville years, "Down on Music Row."

After Dolly became a star, Willadeene, Dolly's oldest sister, published a book about her entitled *In the Shadow of a Song.* She describes those early days of struggle:

> She and Uncle Bill traveled to shows all over Tennessee and to the surrounding states in his old car. Many times Dolly came from shows wrapped in a quilt because her car had no heater and cold air poured in through the holes that had rusted through the floorboard. They always packed sandwiches and a Thermos of coffee and fruit jars filled with tea, because they couldn't afford to buy anything at a restaurant. Dolly would have to shift her position in the seat each time a bump in the road brought a new spring through the upholstery.

The next two years were to be among the hardest of Dolly's life. Although she sold a few of her songs to other artists, they weren't hits, and she couldn't seem to get her career off the ground. Carl, with whom she was in love, went into the U.S. Army, and their courtship was interrupted just when his presence was most necessary to her. She missed her home, and the warmth, love, and approval with which she had always been surrounded. Things just weren't working out the way she had hoped and even expected. It didn't seem as though Nashville had been just sitting and waiting for Dolly Parton to show up.

She stayed with the Owenses for about 6 months,

but after Bill Owens went on the road she moved out and got an apartment of her own, a small, inexpensive place with no telephone and an empty refrigerator. She couldn't afford even a used car to get her to her gigs or make the rounds.

Dolly, who loves to eat and who has fought a weight problem since she turned thirty, was facing a bare cupboard and going hungry for the first time in her life. Many times she has told the story of eating relish and mustard on . . . nothing. That's all there was, and "to this day, I still can't eat a bite of relish." Her weight dropped to 90 pounds. When she visited her family back in Sevier County, they were so horrified by how skinny she was that Dolly came back to Nashville loaded down with flour, sugar, and jars of the fruits and vegetables that Avie Lee pickled and preserved.

Dolly says the only time she ever got a decent meal in those days was when she was out on a date and her companion bought her dinner, but she wasn't doing a lot of dating with Carl in the service. So, while Carl was away, Dolly didn't do a whole lot of eating.

Much worse than hunger pangs was the loneliness she must have felt as she cried herself to sleep every night. Growing up in a two-room shack with two parents and ten brothers and sisters had surrounded Dolly not only with noise, but with comfort and company. She had never had a bed to herself, but that was all right, too.

Now, not only was Dolly alone, without the support of her close-knit family to lean on, but the man she loved was in the service, and they weren't in a position to marry. Long, lonely days and nights for a girl who had never been away from home before.

Working part-time as a waitress, she managed to get singing gigs from time to time, and continued writing songs, alone and with her Uncle Bill. At first, every record company executive in Nashville shook his head no. Then, Fred Foster of Monument Records heard her material and liked it. Soon after Dolly arrived in Nashville, she had left Tree and gone on to sign with Monument Records as a recording artist, but the company didn't really understand how to utilize her.

Dolly's voice is special; it has been described by John Rockwell, a music critic for *The New York Times*, as a soprano that "can shift from eerily accurate girlishness to a weepy little vibrato to a high, hard nasality . . . and she phrases and ornaments like the great artist she is."

Dolly herself says her voice was "so strange, and still is." Monument wanted Dolly to sing a rocking kind of pop that was sweeping the nation, and she says, with typical kindness, "Monument Records was doing what it thought was best at the time. They didn't think I could possibly sell any country because they thought I sounded like a twelve-year-old girl. It wasn't commercial enough for them. They didn't think I could sell any hard-message song or sad story, sing about an unfaithful lover or a cheatin' husband or a busted-up marriage, because nobody would believe it. I guess they thought my voice was so weird that country people wouldn't go for it." Dolly often describes herself as "an acquired taste. You either get used to my singing or you never like it at all."

Dolly wanted to sing country, and only country. Monument wanted rockabilly, an uneasy marriage blend of twangy country and bouncy pop. Meanwhile, she and Bill Owens were under contract to write songs for Monument's publishing company, Combine. Her advance draw was $50 a week against royalties, barely enough to put some food into that empty refrigerator, especially when Dolly was sending money home to the family.

Even though Dolly was frustrated about not being allowed to record her own kind of music— "When you ride the fence you just kind of sit there; I wasn't writing much or choosing any of my own material, and I have to do both to be happy"—she was gaining valuable experience. She was starting to learn how to dress and move like a professional performer, not an amateur, although she still had a long way to go in shaping her image. She was becoming aware of her vocal limitations and how to get around them. And she was getting more used to big-city ways and the ins and outs of the record business.

Nineteen sixty-six was a watershed year for Dolly Parton. Carl Dean came back home from the army and asked Dolly to be his wife. This required serious thought on Dolly's part. She loved Carl; of that she had no doubt, but she loved music, too, and she had no intention of merely settling down into a Nashville kitchen and tying on an apron.

Dolly approached the offer of marriage the same way she approaches everything in life—with straightforward, dead-on honesty. If Carl could accept her as a wife exactly the way she was, a woman with a dream to fulfill, a woman determined to let nothing stop her from success as a writer and entertainer, then she would marry him. But she needed to be free, to be herself, to do what she set out to do, and if that kind of woman stuck in Carl's craw ... well, maybe he should find himself another, more traditional kind of wife.

Carl wanted Dolly. "If that's what will make you happy, that's what it's gonna be," he told her. On May 30, 1966, Memorial Day, just a few days before Dolly's twentieth birthday and two years after they had met, they were married in Ringold, Georgia, and have been married ever since.

They were married in a church, in the presence of Avie Lee Parton, the only member of the family to drive all that way to attend. After the ceremony, the three of them were driving back and had almost reached Nashville when Dolly's mother suddenly discovered that she'd left her pocketbook back in the church. She had put it down on a bench when she snapped the newlyweds' photograph, and had completely forgotten it! That was how they spent most of the hours of the wedding night, driving with Dolly's mother back and forth between Georgia and Tennessee in quest of a handbag.

"I think the Lord intended for me to marry Carl," says Dolly to this day. "I think we were always destined to be together. I just can't imagine being married to anyone else."

The marriage is unique in a number of ways. The more public Dolly became, the more private Carl became. Never did he interfere in her career or attempt to manage her affairs. Instead, he stuck to his own livelihood, asphalt paving, becoming extremely successful at it. They spend most of their time apart, often living in separate houses (Dolly collects residences the way other women collect earrings), and Carl never permits himself to be photographed with his famous wife. He doesn't want to be known as "Mr. Parton," although Dolly takes pride in being known as "Mrs. Carl Dean."

Carl Dean is so private a man that there was a joke going around the Nashville music business that he doesn't actually exist, that he's only a figment of Dolly Parton's imagination. Even today, Dolly still occasionally gets hit with that myth by some enterprising reporter, and always giggles when she hears it.

But Carl and the marriage have been a great stabilizer for Dolly. It has given her a measure of creative freedom that is rare for a woman in a marriage. It has left her free to write songs and make records and films. Her energies are focused elsewhere, on her career, not on her marriage, exactly as she warned Carl before she married him.

"Whenever I'm making a movie or cutting a record, or spending a lot of time on the road, we make up for it when I'm at home. I really think it's been good for the two of us to be away from each other a lot of the time. I'm not sure that this makes any sense, but sometimes you can be closer because you're apart. You're just so happy to see each other and be together, and you don't have time to pick at each other's faults or fight. Carl and I have never had a fight. There's never been any time for one."

Also in 1966, lightning struck. Dolly and Uncle Bill had written a song together, "Put It Off Until Tomorrow," and Bill Owens had taken the demo tape, with Dolly singing, to one of the most important record producers in Nashville, Owen Bradley, who was then with Decca Records. Owens wanted a Decca artist, country star Bill Phillips, to record it.

Bradley listened to the demo and agreed. He liked the song, but he also liked the girl singer, and he made it a stipulation in buying the song that Dolly sing the harmony on Phillips's record. Some versions of the story say it was Phillips himself who heard the song and took it to Bradley, insisting that the girl singer work with him on it. Another version insists Dolly made the recording of "Put It Off Until Tomorrow" with Phillips "by accident."

The last version goes this way: Phillips didn't have the melody down pat, so Dolly sang along with him at rehearsals, to keep the tune straight in his mind. The two of them sounded so good together that when the cut was made, Dolly stayed at the microphone. She was paid as a backup singer, but because of her contractual ties to Monument Records, she couldn't get credit on the label. Even without billing, Dolly was eager to oblige.

The record went into the Top Ten on the country charts, with the song winning a BMI (Broadcast Music Incorporated) Award, Dolly's first, but certainly not her last. Ten years later, at the age of twenty-seven, she would be the holder of 14 BMI awards, as well as many other honors.

People were soon wondering who was the sweet female voice harmonizing on the song. They read the record label in vain, looking for the name that wasn't there. It was a mystery that was to be solved on the air, as the disc jockeys, fielding inquiring telephone calls, informed their audiences of the identity of the "li'l gal singer, Dolly Parton."

Dolly had proved to Monument that she was right—that she *could* sing country, and that audiences would buy it and her. Taking its cue, Monument swung into action, and in 1967 Dolly had a record of her own, a country record, in the stores and on the air. The ironically titled "Dumb Blonde" wasn't even a song she'd written herself —it was by Curly Putnam—but she gave it her all (" 'Cause this dumb blonde ain't nobody's fool"), and it became a hit. Before the age of twenty-one, Dolly Parton had attained her first hit record.

"Dumb Blonde" was followed up by a bouncy, sassy little number, "Something Fishy," a song Dolly had written. In it, she sings about her man's unfaithfulness during "fishing trips," that ages-old excuse. It, too, became an instant hit, and the name and talents of Dolly Parton began to be noticed in Nashville. A deliriously happy Dolly wrote a joyful letter to the folks back home to tell them that her "Dumb Blonde" had risen into the Top Ten nationwide, and that she had gone into the studio to cut an album called *Hello, I'm Dolly,*

which would feature the single "Dumb Blonde."
She promised to send them one when it came out
in a month's time.

But that wasn't all the news she had to report.
Dolly had recorded a song she had written herself, "Something Fishy." She called it "real good."

Dolly Parton was working very hard now, out
on the road playing gigs here and there for small
money, and writing new songs, always composing. She was hoping for success with "Something
Fishy," so that she could get another album out
of it. Other singers were picking up on her material. Hank Williams, Jr., had recorded "I'm in No
Condition," and Kitty Wells, the Queen of Country Music, had decided to record "More Love
Than Sense." Another Owens/Parton tune, "Fuel
to the Flame," had gotten as high as number 7 on
the national country music charts.

Finally! Dolly Rebecca was on her way. Other
artists were starting to record her material, and
she was cutting hit records of her own. She was
earning a reputation as a songwriter of great promise. The name Dolly Parton was becoming familiar to people of influence in Music City, U.S.A.
She had established with Monument the crucial
fact that she *could* record country music, and
that the public *would* buy her records. The dreaded
rockabilly had become a thing of the past.

Very soon she was to team up with the man
who, of all the people in the world, would give the
biggest boost to Dolly's career. Dolly was about to
make that quantum leap over the chasm between
success and stardom. The hand held out to her

across the gap was Porter Wagoner's. Nashville, which had once seemed a million miles away to the young Dolly, and which she declared to be her new home, was about to become her personal property.

# Chapter Four

## Hello, Dolly. Hello, Porter.

I learned a lot from Porter. He
inspired me and I inspired him.

—Dolly Parton

If in 1967 Roy Acuff was the acknowledged King
of Country Music, then Porter Wayne Wagoner
was surely its Crown Prince. What Roy was to
radio, Porter was to syndicated television. A star
for twenty-five years, a regular on the "Grand Ole
Opry" since 1957, he'd had his own nationally
viewed TV program since 1960, "The Porter Wagoner Show." He also took this show on the road,
playing numerous concert dates.

Tall, thin, and ruggedly handsome, a long drink
of country water with a crooked nose and a prom-

inent lower lip, his yellow hair piled high in a pompadour and slicked down with pomade, Wagoner could have been the original model for the Rhinestone Cowboy. Dressed up, he was a sight to behold.

Porter togged himself out in outlandish, exaggerated western suits of the type made by Nudie of Hollywood, fringed and fancy-stitched all over and decorated with bright-colored stones and sequins. A typical Wagoner Wagon Master suit would feature covered Conestoga wagons (a play on his name) and tall cactus plants, all picked out in "jewels." He also sported one with rhinestoned wagon wheels on the shoulders and the sleeves, with a rhinestoned neck scarf to match, and cowboy boots, frequently colored red.

Despite his flamboyant attire, Porter's singing style was down-home and simple, usually accompanied by a steel guitar and a fiddle. He was an accomplished picker. His repertoire of songs was traditional, sacramental, or pure country; he ignored rockabilly and pop, and he leaned heavily on sentimental recitations and favorite songs, on the old-time-religion hymns his audiences loved, and on his country-boy humor. It was this combination of show-biz and good ole boy that had made him a star.

And Porter Wagoner *was* a star, no lie. He had the big audiences, the gold records, the Grammys, and the bookings to prove it.

Norma Jean Beasler, known professionally as Miss Norma Jean, was a bright, peppy blonde. She was the female singer with the Wagon Masters male quartet on Porter Wagoner's syndicated TV show since its inception seven years earlier. She was very popular with Porter's audiences. But now, Norma Jean was quitting to get married and move to Oklahoma, leaving Porter looking for a female singer to replace her. Dolly Parton was one of the girls he thought of.

Porter's background wasn't so different from Dolly's. He, too, had been born dirt-poor, raised on a hillside farm near West Plains, Missouri. Unlike Dolly, who had sloughed her way through high school to earn her diploma, Porter hadn't made it through grammar school. He had had to drop out before seventh grade, in order to get a job and help support the family after his father fell ill.

But being uneducated didn't make Wagoner ignorant; on the contrary, he was as smart as they came, and in 1967 he was on the top of the country heap, with an audience numbering more than 45,000,000 viewers, and with more than 100 television stations carrying "The Porter Wagoner Show," some in prime time. In 1966 he won the Country Song Roundup People's Poll Award for the favorite country television program. Among the many songs he made famous, and which made him famous, were "Satisfied Mind" and "George Leroy Chickasaw."

The show featured an extremely popular hillbilly comic, Speck Rhodes, who milked a lot of laughs out of having no front teeth; a quartet called the Wagon Masters, who dressed in watered-down and not nearly so flashy versions of Porter's famous outfits; fiddler Mack Ma Gaha; and

Buck Trent on steel guitar. And the obligatory female singer, dressed in a frilly country-style long dress of gingham or calico, with nipped-in waist and full skirts over crinolines.

In addition to his TV success, Porter had signed with RCA Victor in 1950, and had been a recording star since 1955, with hits in the Top Ten and even the Top Five on numerous occasions. Even before he teamed up with Dolly, he had won two Grammy Awards, both for religious recordings, *Grand Old Gospel* and *More Grand Old Gospel*. Porter's recorded hit singles included "The Green, Green Grass of Home," "Ole Slewfoot," "The Cold, Hard Facts of Life," "Julie," and many others. He was a top moneymaker, booked for concert appearances more than a year in advance, and somebody who knew how to invest one dollar and see it grow into one hundred.

The success of "The Porter Wagoner Show" in the 1960s and 1970s was the inspiration for the launching of a number of similar country music television programs, such as "Midwestern Hayride" out of Cincinnati, "The Wilburn Brothers Show," which started Loretta Lynn on her way to superstardom, the "Los Angeles County Barn Dance," an important show from California, and a program out of Nashville called "Good Ole Nashville Music," which utilized the talents of a number of "Grand Ole Opry" stars. Country and western was truly entering into a Golden Age; its popularity was not confined to the Southern states alone. Country music was as popular in California and the Midwest as it was in Nashville, Tennessee.

Porter had gotten his start much like Dolly—singing on an early-morning local radio program before he was out of his teens. Radio led eventually to "The Ozark Jubilee" on television out of Springfield, Missouri. That was thanks to Red Foley, Wagoner's mentor, who put the show together and selected Porter as a featured artist.

In 1960, the Chattanooga Medicine Company was set to sponsor a half-hour country music television show, but the star performer they were looking for also had to be the pitchman for their products, which included laxatives, deep-heat rubs, a weight-gain compound, and other such down-home self-medications with wonderfully evocative names like Black Draught and the Wine of Cardui. The firm's calendars were considered so "artistic" that they were found on walls all over the rustic Southland. What Chattanooga Medicine was auditioning for, in addition to musical talent, was sincerity and credibility. All of these qualities they found in Porter Wagoner, whose delivery on the commercials was so good, it made tens of thousands want to run right out and buy the products.

As soon as he got his own contracts from the Chattanooga Medicine Company, Porter signed up Norma Jean, who had been a fellow performer on Red Foley's "Ozark Jubilee." A country star in her own right, Norma Jean was heavily in the running for the unofficial title Queen of Country Music, a title held by Kitty Wells until Patsy Cline took it away from her.

But Patsy had died in 1963, at thirty-one tragically young, in the crash of a private plane that had also taken the lives of "Grand Ole Opry" stars "Hawkshaw" Hawkins and "Cowboy" Copas, The Hillbilly Waltz King. Since then the title had been up for grabs, and Norma Jean's name was frequently mentioned as a worthy successor to Patsy. She was a familiar face and voice; therefore, she became an immediate favorite with the audience of "The Porter Wagoner Show." Add to this her success on records, first with Columbia and later with RCA, and she would be a difficult talent to replace. She had been with the show for seven highly visible and flourishing years.

Now, in 1967, Porter Wagoner found himself suddenly without a girl singer. He began auditions immediately, looking at and listening to established performers as well as hopeful newcomers. What he was seeking was that indefinable something—that combination of looks, talent, and personality that would create a chemistry for the show. He kept coming up empty, and then he thought of Dolly.

Although Porter and Dolly had never met, there had been contact of a kind between them. When Dolly was pounding the pavement trying to sell her songs, she had submitted several to Wagoner, for Norma Jean. Although Wagoner had rejected the songs as wrong for his girl singer, he was impressed by the obvious talent that went into writing them. And now, with two hit single records back to back, Dolly Parton was enjoying a certain celebrity in Nashville. Her songwriting talent convinced Porter, who was no mean songwriter himself, that not only could she sing, but that she might be able to supply new material for the program. So Porter Wagoner picked up the phone.

"I had never seen Porter Wagoner in person," Dolly told Jerry Bailey in her first cover story in *Country Music* magazine, back in 1973. "We were big fans of his back home and watched his show on television. I had met a lot of people, but no stars. He called me one day and told me who he was, and I just couldn't believe it."

By this time Dolly Parton could afford a telephone, and even an automobile. But her success was still so brand-new that it kept surprising her. When she heard Porter Wagoner's voice on her phone, Dolly's first thought, she says, was that he was calling to get some songs for Norma Jean. She had heard through the music grapevine that Norma Jean was high on one of the songs Dolly had sent her. Porter set up an appointment, and Dolly went to keep it, carrying her guitar.

Dolly Parton claims to believe it was her songs that Porter was about to audition, never dreaming it was herself. Yet, it was hardly a secret that Porter Wagoner was looking for a girl singer to replace Norma Jean; he had been auditioning singers for some time then, and it was likely that Dolly Parton's name had come up for the job. If she didn't think he was planning to try her out, she certainly must have dreamed it.

Dolly impressed Porter at once. He thought she was beautiful to look at and that she sang quite well. But what really won him over, he's said many times, was her warmth and her sincerity. "She had the type of genuine, likable personality that I could sell to people on television and in person." Notice the operative word "sell" rather than "present." Porter Wagoner always kept a sharp eye on the monetary value of things.

"Dolly came to my office, but she didn't really know what we were going to talk about," Porter told interviewer Jerry Bailey. "She brought her guitar. And she sang a song for me, a song about everything being beautiful. She had written it. And this song told me so much about her. I knew if a person could sit down and write a song like that, they'd have to have a real soul inside 'em."

When Porter pitched her his offer, to come and be Miss Dolly, the girl singer with "The Porter Wagoner Show," Dolly was first flabbergasted, then, when she had managed to catch her breath, delighted. It would be a giant step up for her, exposure to the 45,000,000 viewers of "The Porter Wagoner Show." She jumped at it, accepting with joy.

Thus started a seven-year relationship that was Dolly's first real big break, the phone call that led her to stardom. From this collaboration would come fame, honors, and a series of smash-hit RCA albums.

But first, Dolly Parton had to make good on the show. It was far from easy, and it didn't come overnight. Filling in for Norma Jean was one of the hardest obstacles Dolly would ever be called on to overcome. Although the money was much more than she had earned before in her life, Dolly found the going rough. Norma Jean had had her own loyal following for seven years, not to mention that Dolly's voice was very different from hers.

Whenever the show played the road, as it often did, Dolly would come out onstage to be introduced and, when she stepped to the microphone, instead of applause, she would hear shouts of "Where's Norma Jean?" and "We want Norma Jean!" It was painful (she described it later as "torture") and all Dolly could do was to grit her teeth and go on singing her heart out, trying her best to win them over, even though more than once she came offstage crying. It was almost a year before audiences began to forget Norma Jean and accept this curvaceous little blonde with the girlish soprano in her place. As Dolly herself says, her beginning months with "The Porter Wagoner Show" were "stepping into big, big shoes."

In the seven years of Dolly's collaboration with Porter—1967-1974—they spent far more time together than Dolly spent with her husband, Carl, a fact of which the press was to make many a mention. But Porter and Dolly were both workaholics, and their rigid schedule kept them as close as chain-gang prisoners linked at the ankles.

For two to three weeks out of every month, they were touring to play dates in Wagoner's elaborately luxurious custom bus. When they weren't picking and singing in local auditoriums, theaters, and concert halls, they were taping "The Porter Wagoner Show," writing and rehearsing songs, or cutting records in the studio.

In 1967, when Dolly joined Porter, society was in ferment; America had committed half a million troops to Vietnam, and antiwar demonstrations were escalating; it was the year of the first Human Be-In in San Francisco, the Summer of

Love and the Monterey Pop Festival, the musical watershed year of *Sergeant Pepper's Lonely Hearts Club Band*; it was the autumn of the March on the Pentagon. Yet, on "The Porter Wagoner Show," business went on as usual, with blond Miss Dolly, for better or worse, replacing blond Miss Norma Jean.

Dolly's salary was $300 a night, which equaled $60,000 a year. This was big money in those days, and even bigger money for a girl from Tennessee whose family didn't even own a two-holer. Dolly really earned her money, because Porter Wagoner was on the road so much, and the show gave so many performances, both live and on TV. Porter was booked for at least 100 live gigs a year, and a great deal of time on the road was spent traveling between engagements. But work was the stuff of life to Dolly Parton—she breathed it, ate it, drank it, and asked for second helpings.

Shortly after she joined Porter's show, Dolly's contract with Monument Records and Combine Publishing expired. It was the right time now for two giant steps. First, she formed Owepar Publishing (for Owens and Parton) with her Uncle Bill Owens, to publish and hold the copyrights for their songs. And she moved over to RCA, Porter's label, where she stayed for the next 20 years. How she did it is a classic Parton story, many times reprinted, but always good for one more telling.

Porter took a demonstration tape of Dolly to RCA, to country star Chet Atkins, who headed up the Nashville studio. Atkins listened to the demo, but shook his head. "Porter, I'm sorry, but that girl just can't sing," he told Wagoner. "I don't think she'd sell a single record, because she just can't sing!"

Porter Wagoner wasn't fazed. "Tell ya what," he replied. "S'pose you take out of *my* royalties every penny she loses RCA, because I believe she *can* sing, and I'm gonna prove it!"

On the strength of Porter's influence alone, RCA signed Dolly, and the rest is history. Not only didn't she lose money, leaving Wagoner's royalties intact, but her first single for RCA, "Just Because I'm a Woman," went to number one on the country charts, selling 150,000 copies. Today, she sells more records for RCA than does rock star David Bowie. Dolly also took on a new manager, Don Warden, who had been managing Porter Wagoner for years.

But what really launched Dolly's career skyward was the series of duet albums she made with Porter, including *Just Between You and Me; Always, Always; Porter Wayne and Dolly Rebecca; Once More; The Right Combination/ Burning the Midnight Oil; Together Always* (an ironic title, given the future); *The Best of Porter Wagoner and Dolly Parton; Say Forever You'll Be Mine; Porter 'N' Dolly; Love and Music; We Found It; Two of a Kind;* and *Just the Two of Us.* Thirteen hit albums in seven years—a remarkable achievement. But all of that was still to come. First, the duo itself had to come into being.

Early in their association, while she was still trying to persuade audiences that she was a fit replacement to walk in Norma Jean's big, big shoes, Porter and Dolly had begun rehearsing songs together, singing duets on the bus going between live engagements. It's been said that he did this to get her over her anxieties and unhappiness; following Norma Jean in front of live, hostile audiences was agony on young Dolly's nerves, and the pressure on both of them was excruciating.

It's also been said that the duets were strictly a commercial idea from the first. But whatever it was, altruism or shrewd business sense, it worked. The harmonic blend of their voices—hers so girlishly sweet and his so masculine, the purity and simplicity of their individual singing styles melting and merging together to form an over-whelming unified sound—was a winning combination from the start. It's as though they had been born to sing duets.

A man and a woman singing country music together was not new. Johnny Cash and his wife, June Carter, were a highly successful duo. Other singing teams included Buck Owens and Susan Raye, Jim Ed Brown and Helen Cornelius, Johnnie and Joni Mosby, Waylon Jennings and Jessi Colter, and Don Gibson and Dottie West. Later, Loretta Lynn and Conway Twitty, George Jones and Tammy Wynette, and other famous duos would cut many hit albums. But Porter had never sung duets with Norma Jean; he'd always been a solo performer. This was as new for him as it was for Dolly, but whatever it was, it worked. Clicking from the very beginning, they hightailed it into the recording studio.

In October 1967, just months after Dolly had joined "The Porter Wagoner Show," they recorded their first duet. The song was Tom Paxton's "The

Last Thing on My Mind," a single. Its success was almost instantaneous, as the record made it into the Top Ten by December. It was followed up at the beginning of 1968 by "Holdin' onto Nothin'." Other smash hits soon came, one after another: "We'll Get Ahead Someday," "Just Someone I Used to Know," "The Pain of Loving You," "Daddy Was an Old-Time Preacher Man" (the song Dolly had written in honor of her grandpa, Jake Owens), "Run That By Me One More Time," "If Teardrops Were Pennies and Heartaches Were Gold," and many others.

Their duo album, *Just Between You and Me*, was on the country charts for a long time in 1968, and in 1969 Dolly and Porter collaborated on a popular album, *Just the Two of Us*, and two big hit singles, "Always Always" and "Your Love."

In 1968, the Country Music Association chose Porter and Dolly as the Vocal Group of the Year, and in 1970 and 1971, Dolly Parton and Porter Wagoner were voted the CMA's Vocal Duo of the Year. In 1969, one of Dolly's most precious and long-held dreams became a reality—after many appearances there, she was asked to be a regular on "Grand Ole Opry." Fame had caught up with her at last, even if she had achieved it as the prettier half of a singing duo rather than as her solo self.

"I'd always wanted that glamorous way of life. I wanted to be in the lights and the glitter and have beautiful clothes and jewels and fat hairdos," says Dolly. Now she had it. But was it going to be enough?

Also in 1969, Dolly Parton wrote the song that

has become a country classic, the song that means more to her than any other, "Coat of Many Colors." It was one of the songs she composed on the Porter Wagoner tour bus, and it became the biggest hit she had written thus far. Of the autobiographical nature of her songs, she has said, "You can clean the hurt out of your own self, and you can also help other people who hurt the same way but maybe can't express it."

Dolly Parton had a number-one single in 1970, "Mule Skinner Blues," and RCA issued a retrospective album, *The Best of Dolly Parton*, which was only moderately successful, but which was to turn gold years later, after her crossover into popular music.

In April 1970, Dolly went back home to Sevierville, but this time she carried no cardboard suitcase filled with dreams and dirty laundry. This time it was to celebrate Dolly Parton Day and receive the keys to the city. She established the Dolly Parton Scholarship Foundation for her old high school, Sevier County High, to aid needy students in obtaining a college education. Dolly was photographed admiring a bronze commemorative plaque with her image on it.

It was a glorious day for Dolly Rebecca Parton, the hometown girl receiving the honors of which she had always dreamed. How proud her parents and brothers and sisters must have been, as speaker after speaker stood up to sing Dolly's praises. The general manager of "Grand Ole Opry," Bud Wendell, was one of the laudatory speakers; another was good old Cas Walker, who had given Dolly Parton her start over station WIVK.

More than 2,500 people turned out for Dolly; in a town the size of Sevierville, that was a mob scene. After a parade that traveled two miles from the town center to the high school, they crowded into the auditorium to watch Dolly record a live LP for RCA. A special bus had brought the band and the engineers down from Nashville. Porter Wagoner made a surprise appearance.

During the presentation ceremonies, BMI gifted her with a set of silver cups. She was a hometown hero; how it must have thrilled her when she looked back on her virtually friendless high school days. The very people who had laughed at her ambitions and her dreams of stardom were now cheering her, and telling one another, "Dolly and me, we was *this* close in high school!"

She went back again to Sevierville in 1971 to play a benefit concert for the high school, as she has done many times since, and there Dolly received a gold disc from BMI for "Just Because I'm a Woman."

In 1971, honors were heaped on Dolly Parton, both as singer and as songwriter. She won two BMI awards, one for "Joshua" and the other for "Daddy Was an Old-Time Preacher Man," the song inspired by her grandfather, the Reverend Jake Owens. *Billboard* named Dolly as the Best Female Songwriter, and she was in the top five in the category of Best Female Vocalist in all the trade papers. She was only twenty-five years old.

Obviously, the combination of Porter and Dolly was working well for both of them. Porter gave Dolly the exposure she needed in TV and to live audiences, and taught her a lot about the music business, information the intelligent girl sopped up and stored away. Dolly gave Porter beautiful songs, her sweet soprano blended with his deep voice, and a new lease on his professional life as part of a team. "Because of my songs, Porter makes money," she was to say later. "Because of Porter, I make money."

They looked very natural together, Porter tall and thin, Dolly short, round, and dimpled, both of them blond, and decked out in sparkly finery. Many of their fans assumed they were man and wife. The press assumed they were lovers, especially when Porter began lavishing gifts on Dolly, including diamond jewelry and a Cadillac. "I have diamond rings for all of my fingers, and all of 'em except for my wedding ring are presents from Porter Wagoner," bragged Dolly.

Were they lovers? Porter and Dolly have denied it, but their constant proximity on the road and in the rehearsal studio, their involvement with their music, the many hours spent in each other's company—with all these taken together, it would have been stranger if they hadn't been.

Still, Dolly insists, "Everybody always thought there was somethin' goin' on between Porter and me, but there wasn't, not sex, anyway. He wasn't my lover or my sugar daddy. A man and woman don't necessarily have to have sex to have a love relationship goin', and I'm not ashamed to say I loved Porter Wagoner. There was a great love and respect between us, and it was a unique relationship, one of a kind. But if we was goin' to bed together, my husband would have been the first to know, 'cause you can't hide a thing like that. I would never hurt Carl that way. Besides, Carl always knows he's the one I love."

A few years after Owepar Publishing was founded, Uncle Bill sold his interest to Dolly. One Christmas during their seven-year association, Dolly either gave to Porter Wagoner (or sold; there is more than one version of the story) a half interest in Owepar, which held the copyrights to the songs she had written with her Uncle Bill Owens and by herself. By now, Uncle Bill seemed to be very much out of the picture, although another of Dolly's uncles, Louis Owens, was at the helm of Owepar.

But, whether gift or sale, Porter and Dolly were now partners in a profitable venture, owning jointly an extensive catalog of songs, including Porter's as well as Dolly's, and a hit list that included "Jolene," "Coat of Many Colors," "Joshua," "Daddy Was an Old-Time Preacher Man," "The Last One to Touch Me," "The Right Combination," "Katy Did," "Burning the Midnight Oil," and many others.

That co-ownership was to prove disastrous to Dolly after she broke with Porter Wagoner. It would lead to bitter recriminations and a multi-million-dollar lawsuit.

Meanwhile, Porter was smoothing out the rougher edges of Dolly's image, grooming her and teaching her a great deal about how to dress for the stage, and how to project her personality to an audience. The first thing he did was to get her out of those frilly dresses and country calicos and glamorize her image to match his own. This was show business, and country music audiences enjoyed the glitzy glamour of tinsel and glitter.

Dolly's appearance kept improving, and her wigs and flashy sequined and jeweled clothing became a female echo of Porter Wagoner's. She even wore tightly fitted custom-made trousers suits with jeweled patterns down the legs, just like Porter's. But where Porter's personal logo was always the wagon or the wagon wheel to match the name of Wagoner, Dolly's became the butterfly, which she had by now adopted as her own symbol, and always wore, often in the form of diamond jewelry given to her by Wagoner. Porter once estimated that during the years of their relationship, he gave Dolly five diamond rings, a diamond necklace, and two Cadillacs. Dolly's little hands were covered by so many rings from Porter that one could barely see the wedding ring from Carl Dean.

Diamonds may be a girl's best friend, but much more important to Dolly was her career as a songwriter. She was writing furiously, song after song spilling out of her thoughts and onto the strings of her guitar. The Porter Wagoner era was the time in which Dolly's creativity reached its zenith—"Coat of Many Colors," "Joshua," which became a number-one chart-topper for her, "I'll Never Stop Loving You." The hits just kept coming, tumbling over one another as though they had waited years to be released from inside Dolly. In 1972, Dolly wrote "Washday Blues" and "Touch Your Woman"; in 1973, "Travelin' Man"; between 1973 and 1974, the great "Jolene." She and Porter collaborated on "Please Don't Stop Loving Me" in the same year, and in 1974, Dolly composed her trademark classic, "Love Is Like a Butterfly." Nineteen seventy-five saw "We Used To" and "The Seeker." Nineteen seventy-six brought forth "Hey, Lucky Lady," "All I Can Do," and, as a duet with Porter, "Forever Is Longer Than Always." There seemed to be no stemming the creative tide; Dolly was pouring the deepest part of herself into her songs.

The relationship between them inspired them both, because Porter Wagoner, who had abandoned his songwriting for almost two decades, began composing again, too.

"She's as creative as anyone I've ever met, including Hank Williams," said Wagoner of Dolly Parton. He spent a lot of time and energy producing her albums. "To me, a record is like a monument," he told Toby Thompson of *The Village Voice*. "Important that it's done right. Dolly's voice is a hard voice to capture on record—very piercing, gives the equipment a fit. . . . I cain't hardly place Dolly in any vocal tradition. She's very unique. I've never known anyone in my twenty-two years with RCA like Dolly at all. I cain't fix our duets in any sort of tradition, either. Our harmony is so close it's almost like blood kin. Brother and sister, you know, can harmonize better than a great tenor and a great lead singer gettin' together. . . . Dolly and I sound nearly like brother and sister."

Hit albums followed one right after the other, most of them showing up on the country music charts, including: 1969—*Blue Ridge Mountain Bow*; 1970—*Best of Dolly Parton, Fairest of them*

*All, Real Live*; 1971—*Coat of Many Colors, Golden Streets of Glory, Joshua*; 1972—*Touch Your Woman, My Favorite Songwriter, Porter Wagoner,* and the duet album with Porter, *The Right Combination/Burning the Midnight Oil*; 1973—*Bubbling Over.*

But there was trouble in paradise.

In 1974, Dolly was no longer the wide-eyed naïve little girl that she had been in 1967. She knew that for every dollar she was earning, Porter Wagoner was earning at least ten. She was twenty-eight years old, and as famous as she had become, she was not yet the star she intended to be. She was *half* a star, half of "Porter and Dolly." Also, Wagoner was going around saying that he had made Dolly Parton a star, that he had created her, and those words chafed.

"He *helped* me become a star, but he didn't *make* me a star!"

But it was Porter's show, and Porter was pulling the strings. Porter handled the business end of things, and made most of the decisions for the two of them. Dolly began to feel like a marionette. Wasn't it *her* songs that were making their duet records such huge hits? Wasn't her talent at least equal to his, and (she thought secretly) even greater? Wasn't she standing poised just at the beginning of her career, while he, much older, was beginning to wind down? Who was riding on whose coattails? And, bottom line, wasn't Dolly Parton's ego every bit as large and every bit as demanding of satisfaction as Porter Wagoner's?

Even in the recording studio, Dolly and Porter weren't seeing eye to eye anymore. As Dolly told her biographer, Alanna Reed, "When he was producing me, I got some of my ideas across and the big part of my ideas were written in the songs, the arrangement ideas and all. But there was so much I wanted to do, and he heard it so differently that we just couldn't agree on so many things. It just took away the joy of me recordin' the song at all. Because then it wasn't what I'd created it to be. It had taken on somebody else's personality. That's hard to explain to people who aren't writers, but without Porter, at least I can write the songs and get them down the way I hear them."

Dolly began to feel choked, locked into a relationship of business and image that restricted her and held her back. She wanted to be Dolly Parton, free to fly, not the soprano side of Porter Wagoner, held to earth. She wanted something that would be entirely her own, with all the fame that could come with solo stardom. In short, she wanted to run her own show.

Money was no small consideration. "Why should I make hundreds *and* thousands, when I can make hundreds *of* thousands?" she demanded, with some justice.

In a clash of wills and temperaments, they began to fight. Porter and Dolly had similar personalities; each was as stubborn as the other, each as set in his own ways. The bloom was off the rose; the magic had gone out of the partnership. Dolly Parton became determined to go it on her own. Porter, it goes without saying, didn't want her to quit the show. He refused his permission, but she went ahead and did it anyway.

For her, it was a natural progression, up and out, leaving Porter Wagoner behind. It was like a spacecraft jettisoning booster rockets when they are no longer necessary, when they keep the craft earthbound, not allowing it to soar free into outer space. Dolly Parton had done it before, and she would do it again. Many great stars behave in this way, always putting their careers above their relationships, and Dolly Parton has never made a secret of it, not even when she married Carl Dean. Career to Dolly—her music and the free expression of it—would always come first in her life.

Porter Wagoner had given her a lot, but now he had nothing left to give. Dolly had learned everything she needed to learn from Porter. She had charmed his audiences and held them in the palm of her small hand. But now she'd outgrown him, and it was time to go on to the next phase of her life, to try her wings . . . solo.

# *Chapter Five*

Good-bye, Dolly. Good-bye, Porter.

> We were good for each other in a lot of ways and just a disaster for each other in a lot of ways. I'll always love him, in my own way. You have to follow your own dreams.
>
> —Dolly Parton

It wasn't a new story by any means; it didn't happen to Dolly Parton alone. A young girl, standing on tiptoes at the beginning of her professional life, needing all the help she can get. A successful man, much older, much wiser, a mentor. A relationship, professional and personal, benefiting both, profitable to both. He teaches her everything he knows, and she proves a willing pupil. But then it goes on for too long. The man is satisfied, but the girl grows into a woman. She discovers she has no identity of her own, but is merely half a team. She longs for that identity, longs to be herself, to be recognized for her own attainments, her own talents. She is certain that by herself she can surpass everything they have accomplished together. She dreams dreams, and she longs to put "legs on them." She struggles to break free and fly like an eagle into the clear blue morning, but the man doesn't want to let her go. Why should he? For him, everything is just fine the way it is. It leads to quarrels, it leads to bitterness, it leads to recriminations, and, eventually, to hatred. The woman gets her way, but the process is not unlike open-heart surgery without anesthesia.

"Porter knew I was plannin' to leave, and he didn't like it one single bit. I tried explainin' things to him, hopin' we could work it out between us, but he wasn't of a mind to listen. He just wouldn't talk to me, and when I saw I wasn't gettin' through to him, I just made up my mind that I was goin' to go the best way I knew how. He wasn't ever gonna give me his permission, so I just took it and left."

Dolly Parton makes it sound so easy, but it was far from simple, cutting the personal and professional ties of seven successful years. It involved lawyers, contracts, and percentages. Porter wasn't merely her singing partner and friend. He was also, by a contract they had both signed in 1970, Dolly Parton's manager and record producer. He wasn't about to let her go without a sizable piece of the future action.

Dolly didn't walk out; she bought herself out. She agreed to a percentage of her recording royalties *in perpetuity*, plus a percentage of her net income for the five years following the split. This was to compensate Porter for the loss of income he would suffer, no longer being her manager and producer.

Yet there would be other kinds of suffering; feelings were bound to be torn to shreds in the break. Breaking up is hard to do, as the song says. When Norma Jean had left his show, Porter had simply gone looking for another girl singer. If he let out any howls of anguish, it wasn't where anybody could hear. But with Dolly Parton it was different. They had been a hit duo, and maybe more. Breaking up with Dolly really hurt. Porter Wagoner would complain that Dolly Parton had used him as a stepping-stone on her way to bigger and better things. Dolly Parton would respond that Porter had gotten his money's worth in the seven years she had been his singing partner, and especially because he produced her albums.

Even after Dolly had announced that she was leaving "The Porter Wagoner Show," even while they were squabbling in private, the two were still singing in public as though nothing had happened. When they concertized in the Civic Auditorium in Oxnard, California, Bob Kirsch of *Billboard* wrote: "Dolly Parton is surely destined for superstardom in the country field, with a beautiful voice and a great writing talent. She has had her share of number-one records, but her material

is becoming more consistently excellent and her
hits are coming with more regularity. . . . Ms. Parton should have no trouble carving a permanent
niche for herself in the country field, even after
leaving the Wagoner show this summer. . . ."

In 1974, RCA released a number of Dolly's
Porter-produced hit albums, including *Jolene* and
*Love Is Like a Butterfly*. But by then, the duo was
in big trouble.

Even Porter Wagoner had to admit that there
had been conflicts between them, on the show
and in the studio. In an interview he gave writer
John Morthland, he said, "We were gonna do
things my way. Because that's the kind of person
I am. Dolly Parton's career up until she left me
was done my way. That's the only way it could
be successful operating with me, because if we
had done it her way it wouldn't have worked.
Had we done the songs she'd have liked to do,
the way she'd have liked to do them, it just would
not have worked. Because I couldn't produce them
that way, first of all, I would not allow them to
be done that way on my show. I signed the checks
at that time, so we did things my way, and that
was the way I was born and reared to do it—that
if you paid a man to work for you, he worked for
you; he didn't tell you what to do. If he did, that
would be called an advisor. I wasn't looking for
an advisor when I hired Dolly. We were using my
ideas, my guidance, and my direction. That's the
way it was."

For Dolly, breaking out of that stifling atmo-
sphere, breaking away from the continual quar-

reling, and breaking up with Porter Wagoner were the next natural upward steps on her ever-ascending ladder to the stars. That decision had probably been in the making ever since she had reached number one on the charts as a solo artist with "Joshua" back in 1970. She was becoming a star attraction.

It wasn't her first such career move; she had left Uncle Bill Owens and Monument Records after Fred Foster had spent time and money fostering her (some $20,000 Monument spent for Dolly's voice lessons was one of the sums bandied about); she would one day leave RCA for Columbia. Success so often involves a series of opportunities taken and people left behind.

But Porter Wagoner was bitter; he has gone on record saying that he had devoted some 95 percent of his time to Dolly Parton, he had spent a fortune on shaping her and molding her, and then he didn't hear from her for a year.

Country music lovers reacted to the breakup of Dolly Parton and Porter Wagoner in the same way that rock 'n' roll fans reacted to the breakup of the Beatles—with shock, horror, and disbelief followed by outrage. The parting of the ways between Porter and Dolly was like a divorce in the family. Dolly's resignation from the show occasioned nearly as much press coverage as the resignations of Israeli Prime Minister Golda Meir, West German Chancellor Willy Brandt, and British Prime Minister Edward Heath, all of which took place in 1974. Those three were merely global leaders, while Dolly Parton and Porter Wagoner were *stars*!

Some people around Nashville were claiming
that Porter and Dolly had had a lovers' quarrel,
but others maintained that the split was much
more about money than about love. More word
had it that Porter Wagoner was: a. fit to kill; b.
broken-hearted; c. jealous. Take your pick of one
or all the preceding. The fact remains, and future
events were to show, that Porter was very op-
posed to Dolly Parton's leaving "The Porter Wagoner Show," and very bitter about what he thought
of as her ingratitude.

In 1978, Dolly told Lawrence Grobel in *Playboy*,
"Porter has been one of the greatest and most
popular country artists of all times. I can never
take the credit away from Porter for givin' me a
big break." But, "We just got to where we argued
and quarreled about personal things. Things we
had no business quarreling about. It was beginning to tarnish a really good relationship. We
didn't get along very well, but no more his fault
than mine. We were just a lot alike. Both ambitious. I wanted to do things my way and he wanted
to do things his way."

Dolly Parton made no secret of the fact that she
felt trapped with Porter Wagoner, but Porter's
angrily bitter retort was, "That trap was pretty
nice to her. There were no complaints at the
beginning. I didn't set the trap to catch her, you
know. It was set in a very humble manner of
'Would you help me get started, 'cause I'm just a
little country girl from east Tennessee who's tryin'
to get started in the country music business as a
singer and songwriter?' But it's awful easy to
convince yourself that 'I'm the only one that can

do this, ain't nobody involved in this but me, and I gotta do it my way.' "

In July 1974, Dolly thought she was ready to do it "her way." When she left Wagoner's show, she was ready to become a superstar, and she couldn't accomplish it working for somebody else. It was the age of "do your own thing," and Dolly's own thing was a need to assert her own creativity and personality and musical ability. She was ready to be a whole entity, not half of one. She was also ready to earn $2,500 a night, which is what she commanded when she started down the solo road.

Nineteen seventy-four was a most important year in Dolly's songwriting career; it was the year she wrote "Jolene," her biggest chart-buster up to then, becoming the number-one country music song in the nation, and an international hit, recorded by Olivia Newton-John and Patti Smith. In the same year, Dolly also wrote "Love is Like a Butterfly," and "I Will Always Love You," which went into the Top Five.

Nineteen seventy-four was also the year she formed her own backup group, the Travelin' Family Band. Since all the Partons are musical, it seemed very natural for Dolly to keep it in the family and select her backup from among those nearest and dearest to her. Dolly spent a year touring with members of the Travelin' Family Band: brother Randy, twins Floyd and Frieda, an uncle, and a cousin named Dwight. It wasn't as good an idea as it sounded; in fact, it turned out to be more of a mistake, something of a false step in her career, but at the outset she was high on the concept of making music with her family.

Dave Hickey interviewed Dolly Parton in a cover story for *Country Music* magazine in July 1974. Dolly told Hickey, "I been getting my band together, lately. Two of my brothers are gonna be in it so we can sing family harmonies. And I'll tell you, however much work it takes to get it right, that's how much I'll do. I'll work myself to death for my music, 'specially for my show. That's what I've always wanted: to be a singing star with my own show.

"Writing and performing," she went on, "they're really my life, and I'm getting more mature about it. I don't run myself into the ground like I used to, staying up for days on the road."

"Now that I'm on my own," she told *Rolling Stone* reporter Chet Flippo, who was to follow her career adoringly, "I'm becoming more of what I really am, instead of having to be just a part of somebody else."

On August 25, 1974, in only her fourth concert appearance after leaving "The Porter Wagoner Show," Dolly was second-billed to Merle Haggard at the Anaheim Convention Center in what *Billboard* said "may well be the California country concert of the year." The trade journal noted that Dolly "was simply outstanding. Given a full hour to do her material, Miss Parton has ample chance to demonstrate all facets of her fine material. . . . Highlights were the excellent 'I Will Always Love You,' 'Jolene,' 'Coat of Many Colors,' 'Sacred Memories,' and the beautiful 'I Believe' encore. As a singer and a writer she is marvelous, and her voice must rank as one of the most distinctive and best in country. Her band is competent. . . ."

In public, Porter and Dolly were still playing kissy-face. Even though she'd left "The Porter Wagoner Show," Porter was still Dolly's record producer, on albums such as *Dolly; The Bargain Store; Best of Dolly Parton;* and *Say Forever You'll be Mine,* the last-named their duet album of 1975. Publicity releases were sent out assuring the press, who in turn assured the public, that Dolly and Porter "were still good friends." Besides, each still had a half interest in the phenomenally successful Owepar Publishing, which had become one of the giants of Music Row in Nashville.

In fact, the official version stated that it was Porter Wagoner who "coaxed" Dolly Parton into becoming a television star in her own right, with her solo TV show, "Dolly!," syndicated on 140 stations, making her, according to the trade journal *Billboard,* "the first female country star to headline such a show." The fact is, even if it wasn't Porter who "coaxed" her—and it was hard to think of Dolly Parton as needing persuasion to do her own TV show—the program was produced by Bill Graham of Show Biz, the same outfit that produced "The Porter Wagoner Show."

The show, simply called "Dolly!," was something of a mishmash. Taped at Opryland in Nashville, it featured a gigantic butterfly as the backdrop to the set designed by Rene Lagler; Dolly's theme song for the show was her hit "Love Is Like a Butterfly."

"Dolly!" had a sizable budget—between $85,000

and $100,000 a show, the largest budget for any
syndicated TV show that ever came out of Nashville. During its 6-month run, the program featured such guests as K. C. and the Sunshine Band,
the Fifth Dimension, and the Hues Corporation,
all of whom were pop and disco favorites, not
country music artists. Dolly even donned a plati-
num-blond Afro wig to sing and dance with the
Hues Corporation. Of course, there were great
country singers on the show, too, like Linda
Ronstadt and Emmylou Harris, Anne Murray, Mel
Tillis, Kenny Rogers, Ronnie Milsap, Tennessee
Ernie Ford, and Tom T. Hall. The childlike Dolly
even had Captain Kangaroo on as her guest, and
poet-singer Rod McKuen. The one guest she longed
for, but who continued to elude her, was Bob
Dylan.

Dolly herself wasn't too crazy about the show;
her favorite ones were those in which she had
her entire family on, pickin' and singin', and the
one where Linda, Emmylou, and Dolly sat quietly
on the stage, their voices harmonizing beautifully, a little foretaste of the great *Trio* album to
come ten years later.

But if Porter Wagoner seemed to be taking pleasure in Dolly's success in public, in private it was
a very different state of affairs. Porter was mighty
displeased with his protégé's actions, and he was
still smarting at her remarks to the press about
not wanting to continue being a part of somebody
else, or that Porter Wagoner hadn't *made* Dolly
Parton a star, but only helped her to *be* one.

Porter wasn't happy about little Dolly leaving
the nest to fly on her own, maybe even to fly

higher than he could. He had spent a lot of time and effort grooming her, giving her half his spotlight, and the fact that Dolly had repaid him a thousandfold wasn't enough. He still accused her of base ingratitude. He simply couldn't understand Dolly Parton's overwhelming need to go it on her own, find her own place in the sun.

Whenever Dolly was quoted in a newspaper or magazine as saying things like Porter Wagoner was one of the greatest country music stars in history, and how he gave her her big break, and how grateful she was and how she would never, ever take a lick o' credit away from him, but . . . Porter would become righteously indignant. He felt she was already patronizing him, downgrading him by "making nice" in public, as though he were a child.

"I'd be less than truthful," Porter told Country Style magazine, "if I said I wasn't disappointed in the way the relationship turned out. I put a lot of energy into making her records great and my own records suffered."

The rift between Dolly and Porter was to widen; misunderstandings and anger would increase, charges and countercharges would be hurled, until finally their partnership would dissolve in mutual recriminations.

The trade journals tell the whole sad story: From Variety, 8/25/76: PARTON, WAGONER DISSOLVE VENTURES Nashville—The click country music team, Porter Wagoner and Dolly Parton, have officially dissolved all of joint business ventures. The pair, together since 1966 [sic], decided in 1974 to bill Parton separately from "The Porter Wagoner Show," although Wagoner still produced her records. Parton has now signed with a West Coast management agency and plans to produce her own records, relieving Don Warden as manager. The business aspects concerning the publishing of songs and a Wagoner-Parton-owned publishing firm have yet to be resolved.

From *Billboard*, 3/31/79: DOLLY PARTON HIT WITH $3 MIL SUIT. Nashville—Porter Wagoner has slapped his one-time partner and protégé Dolly Parton with a $3 million lawsuit.

Alleging breach of contract, the suit was filed Wednesday in Chancery Court for Davidson County, Tenn.

Wagoner filed the suit individually and doing business as Porter Wagoner Enterprises, and on behalf of Owepar Publishing Co. Defendants are Dolly Parton Dean (her married name), individually and as an officer and director of Owepar Publishing, and doing business as Velvet Apple Music, Song Yard Music, and Dolly Parton Enterprises.

The action seeks an accounting of all Parton's net income and record royalties to the date of judgment, 5% of her net income from June 1974 through June 1979, and 15% of her record royalties from the date the payments ceased to the date of judgment. Wagoner also wants the court to issue a declaratory judgment that Parton "is liable under contract to pay Porter Wagoner 15% of her record royalties earned from the date of judgment for so long as she receives such record royalties."

As an alternative to the above demands, Wagoner seeks $2 million for "future loss of income from Dolly Parton Dean's net income and record royalties."

From *Variety*, 3/28/79: GOOD-BYE DOLLY IS WORTH $3 MIL IN WAGONER SUIT Hollywood—Dolly Parton's former singing partner, producer, and manager, Porter Wagoner, has filed a $3,000,000 breach-of-contract suit against the singer, claiming that she has failed to make certain payments to him since their 1974 breakup.

Parton and Wagoner ended a seven-year partnership in July, 1974, after recording a series of albums together and performing as a duo on Wagoner's TV series and in concert. Wagoner also produced Parton's solo albums during that period.

According to the suit, filed in Nashville Chancery Court, Wagoner agreed to free her from a 1970 contract in exchange for a percentage of her recording royalties in perpetuity, as well as a percentage of her net income for the five years following the split. The sums were to compensate for Wagoner's loss of producer's royalties and his loss of future income as her manager.

The suit seeks 15% of her net income from June, 1974, through June, 1979, and 15% of her recording royalties forever, or a flat

$2,000,000 payment. Wagoner also seeks $1,000,000 for loss of producer's royalties during the June 1974–June 1979 period.

The suit also asks for the return of some 130 songs which were part of Parton and Wagoner's joint music publishing company, Owepar. . . .

The lawsuit was to drag on for years, growing more and more bitter, making only the lawyers rich, until it was settled out of court for an unspecified amount.

Meanwhile, from 1974 through 1975, Dolly was doing her syndicated TV show and going on the road with the Travelin' Family Band. And writing songs. In 1975, she turned out "The Seeker," "We Used To," and "The Bargain Store," all of which were produced on albums for RCA by Porter Wagoner.

But if her career as a songwriter was zooming higher than ever, her career as a soloist had taken a backward step. The Travelin' Family Band was nobody's idea of backup heaven; there was an amateurish quality about the entire show that was disappointing to Dolly's fans, who were used to the gloss and polish of "The Porter Wagoner Show."

When Dolly played the Felt Forum in New York City in September 1974, two months after the split with Wagoner, she couldn't bring in enough audience to fill the theater. Top-billed with Bobby Bare and Ronnie Milsap, she apparently didn't have, according to *Variety*, "the pop spillover needed to sell out in Gotham. The second season of country concerts at the Felt Forum got off to a good artistic start . . . but proved a box office dud. Only slightly more than half the 4,500 seats were filled for the show, which headlined Dolly Parton, who looked and sounded great, but whose set was a bit too long.''

John Rockwell of *The New York Times* was equally impressed with Dolly. In an often-quoted review of the concert, he wrote, "Country in New York got off to a rather disappointing season . . . the Felt Forum was nowhere near full. . . . But if the concert was a commercial disappointment, it was nothing like that from an artistic standpoint— at least so far as the headliner, Dolly Parton, is concerned. . . . She is an impressive artist. Her visual trademark is not far from that of Diamond Lil: a mountainous, curlicued bleached-blond wig, lots of makeup, and outfits that accentuate her quite astonishing hourglass figure.

"But Miss Parton is no artificial dumb blonde. Her thin little soprano and girlish way of talking suggest something childlike, but one quickly realizes both that it is genuine and that she is a striking talent; she really is a young woman from the Smoky Mountains of east Tennessee with a strong family sense and allegiance to the basic American rural virtues. . . .''

On the other hand, a loudly dissenting voice was heard from Nick Tosches, a music writer for *The Village Voice*, who reviewed her performance grimly: "There is a darker, more dismal side to Dolly Parton; I went to her recent show at Felt Forum, expecting at least a taste of her proven abilities. Instead I witnessed one of the shoddiest routines this side of 'Hee Haw.' Since she split from 'The Porter Wagoner Show' earlier this year, Dolly has been touring with her own band, made up mostly of relatives. Without exception, the group is third-rate. The lousy music is complemented by Dolly's feigned stupidity; she shucks and gee-whizzes and flutters her baby blues. . . . And let's not forget that painfully obligatory gospel number. . . . All the nonsense that Dolly steers clear of in her writing and recording, she dives into in her live performances. . . . Until Dolly abandons the ersatz yokelisms, her live performance will remain a mere travesty of her worth, not to mention bad. What she is capable of doing with words and sounds is 'act' enough."

Among Dolly's engagements in 1975 was the Waterloo Music Festival, a country music jamboree held in Stanhope, New Jersey, a beautifully restored town dating back to the days of the American Revolution. She wasn't even the sole headliner; Dolly and Gary Stewart, who had a new, successful album out, shared that honor. John Rockwell, the popular-music critic for *The New York Times*, reported on the concert, headlining his piece "A Beguiling Dolly Parton Sings at Jersey Festival."

Rockwell enjoyed Dolly's music, but the act with the Travelin' Family Band left him cold. He called her "a country singer and songwriter of enormous individuality and charm. She retains all of that in concert, but seems more quintessentially country than ever. . . . Her performance was pretty much like any other Parton performance: superb music mixed with canned corn. . . .

Leonore Fleischer

She is doing things she has done innumerable times before. The patter is often appallingly corny. . . .''

Yet, Rockwell easily perceived the great source of Dolly Parton's musical strength and artistry. "Miss Parton's songs deal mostly with her own memories. But her poetry has such a range of emotion and such a truth to it that—as always happens with the best art—the very specificity of her imagery becomes universal." *Universal imagery*—it must have been words like those, so often spoken and written about her work, that made Dolly Parton determined to broaden her horizons and reach out to larger audiences.

During 1974 and 1975, Dolly Parton was busy, but she was far from happy. Now she had the freedom to go wherever she chose, but she seemed to have chosen the wrong direction. She appeared to be "spinning her wheels," not making the progress she had expected. She wasn't satisfied with her management; her backup band, the Travelin' Family Band, hadn't worked out as she had expected; she didn't care for the quality of her TV show. "The show isn't me," she complained, and, after taping 26 shows, production stopped. She was still be be seen on occasional TV shows, such as the October 1975 network special marking the fiftieth anniversary of "Grand Ole Opry." Dolly, dressed in a bright pink tight-fitting pantsuit covered with a pattern of hearts outlined in rhinestones, appeared with the greats of country music, including Loretta Lynn and Roy Clark.

In 1975, Dolly Parton had a banner year for honors and awards. She was chosen by the Country Music Association as Female Vocalist of the Year. She was named Best Female Vocalist not only by *Billboard*, but also by *Cash Box* and *Record World*, trade publications of major importance in the music business. *Billboard* also selected Dolly as Best Female Singles Artist and Best Female Songwriter. She was beginning to amass quite an impressive collection of engraved plaques, cups, and framed citations to hang on her walls.

Yet, except for the record albums and the composing, nothing seemed to be going right. It was time for some major career moves. It was time for a whole new set of decisions that would carry Dolly Parton in an entirely new direction. It was time for what country music historians will always refer to as "Dolly Parton's crossover."

# *Chapter Six*

## Dolly Crosses Over

I'm still the same Dolly Parton.
I'm not leaving country; I'm taking
it with me.

—Dolly Parton

By 1976, although other artists had recorded
Dolly's best songs—star performers as diverse in
style as Linda Ronstadt, who recorded "I Will
Always Love You"; Maria Muldaur, who did a
version of "My Tennessee Mountain Home";
Emmylou Harris, who sang wonderfully "Coat of
Many Colors"; Olivia Newton-John, who had cho-
sen to record "Jolene"; Nancy Sinatra and Lee
Hazelwood, Merle Haggard and even Patti Smith,
who had also cut "Jolene"—Dolly herself still

hadn't broken through with that million-copy seller, the platinum record.

Her own version of her biggest hit to date, "Jolene," had sold about 200,000 copies, which is monster sales in the country charts, but which left Dolly Parton dissatisfied. The admiration and respect of her peers and her country music fans were no longer enough; Dolly Parton's ambitions needed an even bigger pond in which to swim as an even bigger fish. She wanted to reach a lot more people and make a lot more money. "No matter how country you are, you hope for a cross-over hit," she said. "Why not? There's more money and recognition involved. Why are most of these people working, if not for that?"

Dolly Parton was beginning to make a name for herself outside the country milieu. Important journalists on the music scene, like rock 'n' roll writer Chet Flippo of *Rolling Stone*, to whom country music was still something of a sacred subject, discovered her and wrote long, rhapsodic pieces about her and her musicality. There were interviews in major media spots, not the least of which was the long story about Dolly written by Chris Chase for the Sunday magazine of the august and staid *New York Times*.

Chase, who went on to become the biographer of Rosalind Russell and Betty Ford, was captivated by the Parton sound. "Her voice is an amazement," she wrote in the *Times* Sunday magazine, after watching a country music concert at the East Burke High School outside Hickory, North Carolina, where Dolly and the Travelin' Family Band shared the bill with headliner Merle Haggard.

"She has said she sounds like a child 'with grown-up emotion,' but there's more to it than that. In 'Love Is Like a Butterfly,' Dolly's work is itself as sheer and delicate as a butterfly's wings; she skitters over the surface of the words, barely touching them, while in 'Travelin' Man' she hoots and hollers and drives and mocks. Sometimes she hits a high note and it breaks into pieces, and a little shower of crystally sounds comes down; sometimes she hits low notes soft and furry and filled with loneliness. Her voice can quiver, pure and tremulous, or it can twang flat like a banjo string; it can throb, it can lift, it takes an octave jump with foolish ease, and it is almost always true and sweet."

When the same Merle Haggard show played the Anaheim Convention Center in Orange County, California, a Mecca for country music fans, *Variety* reviewed it. The show business bible said that the Travelin' Family Band "ably backed up Parton, but was only passable on its own." But of Dolly herself, *Variety* stated, "Dolly Parton clicked with her hour's worth of material."

Good press, no matter how soothing to the ego, was not the stuff of which Dolly's dreams were made. What Dolly dreamed of was the whole ball of wax, tied up in silver ribbons. She wanted to step out of the confinement of the "country" label. Instead of Best Female Country Music Entertainer of the Year, she wanted her albums to be numero uno on the pop charts in addition to the country charts. She wanted to do television shows that weren't merely syndicated locally in country markets, but big prime-time hits in the big cities, too. She wanted to play Las Vegas. She wanted to make films. To do any of that, to break into the big time, she would have to change. To achieve her larger ambitions, Dolly Parton would have to take the biggest risk of her professional career, even greater than the one she took when she left Porter Wagoner to go solo.

There had been rumblings and speculation about Dolly going pop and breaking away from country as early as 1976, because her TV show, "Dolly!," included pop guests as well as country stars, and Dolly sang right along with them. Were significant changes in the offing? But, when Dolly won Best Female Vocalist of the Year for the second year running at the nationally televised 1976 Country Music Awards, she came onstage with just a simple banjo and sang a mountain ballad of her own, "Applejack," with a sound that was pure Tennessee.

A few weeks later, when she went into the studio to record "Applejack," she was backed up by such "Grand Ole Opry" stars as Minnie Pearl, Kitty Wells, Roy Acuff, Wilma Lee and Stoney Cooper, Chet Atkins, Ernest Tubb, Carl and Pearl Butler, and her own mama and daddy, a group of people she called "the best. They are my greatest inspiration."

Now was the ideal time for her to think things over and make plans. By the middle of 1976, Dolly was exhausted, worn out from going on the road with the Travelin' Family Band, and her vocal cords were beginning to trouble her. This was an ailment that would continue to plague her for years. Heavy tensions were developing in her relationship with Porter Wagoner.

The two of them were very much alike, as Dolly would be the first one to admit, both stubborn and bull-headed. "He won't accept things sometimes the way they are. I won't either, sometimes." As the tangled legalities between them grew more complicated, with Dolly wanting to buy back her song catalog from Porter, and Porter wanting his royalties from Dolly, the situation worsened. Not only did they stop speaking to each other, they stopped seeing each other.

It was obvious to Dolly that things were not working out as she had expected when she went off on her own. For one thing, the Travelin' Family Band would have to go. They simply weren't good enough, and were cramping Dolly's style. She needed an entirely different image; no more would she be Daisy Mae backed up by a bunch of Li'l Abners. Before she'd be ready to widen her horizons and tackle the much more lucrative crossover market, she would have to have more polish and some sophistication. And she needed national exposure to middle-of-the-road audiences. These were things with which the Travelin' Family Band couldn't help her; in fact, they were one of the stumbling blocks in her way.

Her health came first, though, because Dolly's throat was in serious trouble. She had nodes growing on her vocal cords; they were not painful, but did cause hoarseness and a loss of voice. Worse, the voice loss could possibly become permanent. "A node," reported Dr. Edward A. Kantor, "is a small tumefaction—like a rounded corn—on the

Just a pair of pickers — that's Carol Burnett on the banjo.

(Nancy Barr/ Globe Photos)

Dolly Parton at Opryland, as free and as pretty as a butterfly.

(Nancy Barr/ Globe Photos)

Dolly Parton — Here I
Come Again!

(Nancy Barr/
Globe Photos)

Another key to another
city — Dolly conquers the
Big Apple with a free
concert at Mayor Ed Koch's
city hall.

(Zelin/Globe Photos)

Dolly Parton and
Porter Wagoner —
their seven-year
collaboration made
her a star.

(Phototeque)

Tara, Dolly's
23-room dream house
outside Nashville.

(Norcia/
Globe Photos)

Dolly with her Grandpa Jake Owens, the hellfire reverend.

(Norcia/Globe Photos)

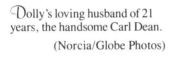

Dolly's loving husband of 21 years, the handsome Carl Dean.

(Norcia/Globe Photos)

Avie Lee and Robert Lee Parton — Dolly's beloved mama and daddy.

(Norcia/Globe Photos)

*Above,* a very famous trio: Linda Ronstadt, Dolly, Emmylou Harris with George Merlis.

(Globe Photos)

The movie they should have left on the cutting room floor. Sylvester Stallone and Dolly Parton in *Rhinestone.*

(Phototeque)

Dolly's "Tennessee mountain home."
(Norcia/Globe Photos)

Dolly Rebecca at home with her family in Sevier County.
Dolly is at the extreme left in the back.

(Norcia/Globe Photos)

"The most painful thing" Dolly had ever done was to make *The Best Little Whorehouse in Texas* with Burt Reynolds, *left*.

(Phototeque)

"Not one bad moment on the whole picture." Lily Tomlin, Jane Fonda, and Dolly Parton star in *Nine to Five*, *right*.

(Dominguez/ Globe Photos)

Two megastars — Dolly with Neil Diamond, *left*, at the party after her successful Amphitheatre opening, September 22, 1979.

(Nancy Barr/ Globe Photos)

"The Mountain Sidewinder" — a one-of-a-kind family fun machine at Dollywood.

(Globe Photos)

vocal cord, a swelling or growth. It is noncancer-
ous, benign. But it's still something you have to
check; hoarseness for more than six weeks is can-
cer until proven otherwise."

Dolly's doctors warned her that if she didn't
give her vocal cords a long rest so that the growths
would have a chance to soften and recede, the
long-developing nodes might have to be removed
surgically. Not only is vocal-cord surgery risky
and painful, involving an operating microscope,
but there are no guarantees that the nodes won't
reappear or that the vocal cords won't thicken as
they heal. Sometimes the vocal color is altered or
even lost entirely. Dolly opted for a long rest.

The first thing she did was to cancel a large
number of road engagements and concerts, 65
concerts, worth $325,000, set up for the months of
June through October, and go "into seclusion."
"Seclusion" meant no interviews and no public
appearances. Dolly didn't even talk, but kept a
pad and pencil by her side with which to communicate. Meanwhile, she was doing some heavy
thinking and mulling over a lot of high-powered
advice, much of it from her friend Mac Davis,
who had successfully crossed over into pop-rock,
and who had enjoyed his own prime-time TV
variety specials.

No doubt, while she was paying attention to
the practical side of things and crunching the
numbers, she was at the same time praying to the
Lord for guidance and for the strength to make
these heavy decisions and carry them out. "I don't
know what it is with me and God," she has said.
"I'm just totally aware of Him. I talk to Him just

like I talk to you. If something's going wrong I'll talk to Him about it. In my heart He's a true friend.

"The joy of living is just doing what you really want to do," she has said many times, and by now Dolly was pretty sure of what she really wanted to do. She wanted to move in a new direction, free her creative drives to take her wherever they went, without the restrictions of strict labeling such as "country music." She wanted to be more than a country artist; she wanted to be an artist, period.

Other country stars before Dolly Parton had attempted to cross over into the pop-rock market, with limited success, like Johnny Cash. Other country stars after Dolly Parton would attempt to cross over, also with limited success, like Crystal Gayle or Tanya Tucker, Ronnie Milsap, Tammy Wynette and George Jones, Loretta Lynn and Conway Twitty.

But some had it all—Linda Ronstadt, Willie Nelson, Mac Davis, Waylon Jennings, Kenny Rogers, Kris Kristofferson—these are a few names that come to mind, singers whose records sell to pop-rock fans as well as to country fans. And there was Bob Dylan, who had crossed in the other direction, and whose sound by now was real country.

The gulf between success and failure, it seemed to Dolly, could be bridged only by effective management. Certainly, the artists who hadn't made it were as talented as those who had; it was sound professional guidance that had made the major difference. Dolly Parton needed jet fuel to rocket her to the top instead of the super-unleaded she had now. And that meant moving the base of her operations from Nashville, Tennessee, to Los Angeles, California, a move that Dolly knew would be looked on by country music fans as "The Great Betrayal." She began to shop around for new management, new representation, and new musicians.

Before Dolly made any announcement of her future change in direction, rumblings were heard as far west as Beverly Hills and as far north as New York City. It is hard to keep major career moves a secret. John Rockwell, pop music columnist and critic of *The New York Times*, was an ardent Dolly fan who had told his big-city readership about Dolly Parton before. Rockwell had interviewed Dolly back in August 1975, when she came with the Travelin' Family Band to play the Waterloo Music Festival in New Jersey. At that time, Rockwell wrote that ". . . there doesn't seem to be much likelihood that she will or could change her image of her music to fit a broader audience's expectations. What is more likely is that the sheer quality of the music and the irresistible charm of the person will win her a wider audience on her own terms."

Although Rockwell couldn't foresee change then, others did, especially in Nashville, and it disturbed them. "People kept tellin' me that I was goin' pop," said Dolly, "but they just plain didn't understand. Everything just got blown right out of proportion. I could hardly believe it. I was changing things that weren't right in my organization, not myself. How could I change myself?

And what would I change into, anyway? A pumpkin at midnight? Naw, I'm so totally me it would scare you to death!"

Her extensive road tour, her television appearances, and the long studio sessions recording her hits had taken their toll, working their damage on Dolly's delicate vocal cords. The node problem that dogged her so painfully was the same one experienced by other singers—Elton John, Neil Young, Fleetwood Mac's Stevie Nicks, to name only a few. Once more, Dolly Parton had to cancel concert bookings, and early in November 1976 RCA records announced to the press that Dolly Parton's doctor had ordered "a long vocal rest, at least through the end of the year." Dolly was forced to cancel at least 25 concerts, and once again to limit her talking.

Alarmed, *Times* columnist John Rockwell telephoned Dolly for an interview. The combination of her illness and the rumors about the impending crossover led to the interview, which Dolly managed to give him over the phone despite the swollen nodes on her vocal cords.

"Dolly Parton is at the brink of a radical shift of direction, one that should, if there is any justice in the pop-music heaven, make her one of the great stars of American entertainment," Rockwell wrote prophetically. ". . . Although she doesn't like to dwell on the subject, it's clear that Miss Parton believes that emotional strain may be partly the cause of her throat problems. 'Any time you make a change,' she worries, 'you gotta pay the price.'

" 'I'm grateful to Porter, I'm very proud of all the

120

things we've done before. But I'm just so proud of the new things. A lot of country people feel I'm leaving the country, that I'm not proud of Nashville, which is the biggest lie there is. I don't want to leave the country, but to take the country with me wherever I go. The truth is, I am country. I am Dolly Parton from the mountains, that's what I'll remain. If people outside want my music, then I'll do my best. If you ask me if I'm pop, I can only be Dolly Parton, and that's country.'

"Miss Parton peppers her conversation now," concluded Rockwell, "with phrases like 'a totally free feeling,' 'there are really no limits now,' and 'after the first of the year, when my new life begins.'"

The storm of protest that greeted her new career decisions was even louder and angrier than she had expected, louder and angrier than that raised at the breakup of Porter and Dolly. Going solo was something her fans could understand, even if it pained them, but going Hollywood? Leaving country music for slick pop with its lush arrangements or even, God forbid, rock 'n' roll or brassy disco? The country music press assailed her, and letters poured in from anguished fans everywhere, begging, pleading, cursing, and threatening.

"I'm still the same Dolly Parton," she reassured her fans. "I'm not leaving country; I'm taking it with me." She also said, "Country music is like a family that should be held together. If somebody is country-oriented and can still appeal to a rock audience, like a Waylon Jennings or a Kris Kristofferson, this is great. But it's important that the audiences know where your roots are. You can be country and pop at the same time if people know where you're really coming from.''

And she proceeded with her plans, disregarding all the advice to the contrary, well meaning and not. She wanted a full, new "now" sound, one that would combine with the story-songs she wrote to bring them within the range of a much larger audience.

# *Chapter Seven*

## Dolly Goes Hollywood

Attention ain't affectin' me none.
My life is exactly the same as when
I was settin' out.

—Dolly Parton

The Los Angeles management firm of Katz Gallin Cleary was the one Dolly Parton selected to help launch her on her new career. Not only did they handle Mac Davis, but, along with other entertainers such as Anthony Newley, Florence Henderson, Paul Lynde, and Joan Rivers, Katz Gallin Cleary managed such vocal artists as Olivia Newton-John, Cher, the then very popular Tony Orlando and Dawn, Donny and Marie Osmond, Gregg Allman, Thelma Houston, and the Amazing Rhythm Aces. It was no less a coup for Katz Gallin Cleary than for Dolly herself when they signed the management contracts.

As she signed them, Dolly made other major changes. She switched her booking agency from Top Billing to Monterey Peninsula Artists, a California firm that booked such top-grossing acts as Carole King, The Eagles, Chicago, and Cheech and Chong. At the same time, she took on International Creative Management, the monolithic ICM.

Much more important, she went to RCA and told them she was going to produce her next album, *First Harvest, New Gathering,* herself. That left Porter Wagoner, who was still producing her albums, out of a job and icily furious. He had only just finished producing her latest-released album, *Bubbling Over,* and was still working on *Bargain Store,* and *All I Can Do.* Not only that, but Dolly also announced that in the future she would be finishing the recording of *New Harvest, First Gathering* in Los Angeles, not Nashville.

At this time, Dolly formally and completely broke away from all her former business ventures with Porter Wagoner. Her album, *All I Can Do,* released in 1976, was the last album he would produce for her. It contained some beautiful songs, among them "When the Sun Goes Down Tomorrow," "Shattered Image," "I'm a Drifter," and a plaintive ballad, "Falling Out of Love with Me," in which Dolly wrote that she had "left while love was still alive," because she didn't want to stay "and watch it die." Did she mean Porter Wagoner? From that point on, Dolly would be her own producer; at most she would co-produce.

"My work is very important to me. I take such pride in it. It's self-expression to me, really my way of being what I am. Lately I've found such happiness and new inspiration in being able to have the freedom to do what is so totally me. I'm writing more and better than ever," she declared. "It's still the same Dolly Parton, but I feel I'm ready to fly. I'm really a pretty brave little number."

The next decision Dolly Parton made when she came out of "seclusion" was that the Travelin' Family Band had to go. They simply were too cornball, too full of what Nick Tosches had called "yokelisms," too hillbilly for the new image that she and Katz Gallin Cleary were about to spring on the world. As musicians, they were barely adequate, nothing more. They had received bad or so-so reviews, had been called "merely competent," and had played to unfilled auditoriums.

Naturally, the press had a field day with this one.

"They made it sound like I had fired my family," complained Dolly, hurt, to *Playboy*'s Lawrence Grobel. "I didn't fire my family, and it hurts me for anybody to say so. I was goin' through a very rough time—poor lighting, poor sound, poor management, poor everything. I just decided I was goin' to quit for a few days, just stop everythin' and do some thinkin'. Because I won't let somethin' run me to a psychiatrist or to a doctor; I can take care of my own things; me and the Lord can talk it over."

To others, Dolly protested, "I had brothers and sisters and cousins in my band. How could I fire them?" Nevertheless, that was the end of the Travelin' Family Band, and the beginning of Gypsy

Fever, a much more professional backup—"more versatile and qualified" musicians, not necessarily from Nashville—with a big pop-rock-country sound. However much she protested she hadn't, Dolly actually *had* fired her family.

"I decided to change so I could expand my music," Dolly told interviewer Stanley Mieses in *Melody Maker*. "I just know I have a lot more music in me than I've ever known, and I just wanted to be able to say, 'Leave me alone to become whatever I want to become.' You hafta understand that it wasn't the fans who were telling me to change. I found myself ruining my voice, playing in places that didn't have good microphones, places that had no class at all, killing myself, knocking myself out night after night. And there wasn't all that much money in it, neither. You can't make a lot of money in country music unless you're a real superstar, and I knew I could make more than I was makin', a lot more."

As Dolly lined up at the starting gate, ready to make the move she would call "the smartest thing I ever done in my life," Katz Gallin Cleary set up a publicity barrage the likes of which Dolly had never seen before. They snagged for her the cover of *Rolling Stone* and the cover of *Playboy*, on which she appeared coyly dressed in a Playboy Bunny suit, revealing that awesome cleavage.

Dolly Rebecca Parton made the cover of *People* for the first, but not the last, time. Katz Gallin Cleary booked her on all the major national talk shows, those of Dinah Shore, Merv Griffin, Mike Douglas, "Hee Haw," "The Today Show," and the rest. You name the show; Dolly was cracking her good-ole-girl jokes on it. Most important, Dolly made her debut on The Johnny Carson program, the "Tonight Show," the present-day equivalent of playing the Palace.

At first, there was some concern in the halls of Katz Gallin Cleary about Dolly Parton's larger-and-sparklier-than-real-life presentation, her gaudy rhinestoned clothes, tight bodices bursting with cleavage, diamonds winking from every finger, those huge preposterous wigs. Should her physical image be softened for the middle of the road? There was anxiety about how she would appear to a non-country audience. How would she go over with the savvy late-night viewer of "The Tonight Show"?

The less sophisticated country people were comfortable with spangles and glitter; they were accustomed to it; they even expected it. Many cowboy singers were flamboyant, like Porter Wagoner, who wore rhinestones and custom-made suits from Nudie of Hollywood. Female country singers were flamboyant, too, often dressing as cowgirls with heavily fringed jackets and skirts and tall, "jewel"-encrusted boots. It was an accepted look. But how would Johnny Carson and his public react? Would Dolly Parton become a national laughingstock on "The Tonight Show"?

Stubbornly, Dolly Parton was not yet ready to tone down her look for city sophisticates. She adored all her baubles, bangles, and beads, and was in no hurry to give them up. Besides, she reasoned, "First, you have to get their attention." Dolly's was an attention-getting show-biz way of dressing. Why shouldn't city folk dig it as much as country folk? She wasn't afraid of going on the

Carson show gaudily decked out in all her jeweled Christmas tree finery, because, as she said, "I work best one to one. I was a fan of Johnny Carson's and I wanted people to notice me. I didn't care if it was for the right reasons or the wrong reasons at first. I felt I had a gift as a writer. I may not be a great singer, but my voice is different. I'm secure in those areas."

Katz Gallin Cleary needn't have worried. Dolly's instincts turned out to be right as country rain; Dolly Parton's overblown way of dressing became her most recognizable trademark in the crossover, and the city slickers loved it. Just as Johnny Cash was always identifiable as The Man in Black, Dolly Parton was identified as the blonde in the wigs and the rhinestones, the gal with the huge boobs.

Dolly Parton's first appearance with Johnny Carson on "The Tonight Show" was a memorable one. It took place on January 19, 1977, Dolly's thirty-first birthday. She sang "Higher and Higher" and "Me and Little Andy," her little-girl-voice song in which an abandoned child and a puppy die and head for Heaven together, which brought tears to everybody's eyes. She told stories about her childhood, laced with her earthy humor. She made jokes about her clothing, the poverty of her Tennessee childhood, her "invisible" husband, the size of her chest, although as usual she declined to give out her measurements, inviting the public to guess.

The Parton quick wit and down-home frankness, her outlandish clothing and wonderful singing, so captured Johnny and his audience that

Dolly became a frequent, favorite guest. In fact, she turned up visiting on so many talk shows that one couldn't switch on the set without encountering those dimples, that Tennessee twang, and those oh-so-recognizable breasts.

A late-night sitcom, very popular with sophisticates, was Norman Lear's "Mary Hartman, Mary Hartman," starring Louise Lasser in pigtails. One of the leads, Mary Kay Place, played Mary's next-door neighbor Loretta Haggars, a country music singer and songwriter whose ambition was to be as famous as Dolly Parton, so that she could go to Nashville and buy outlandish clothing "just like Dolly's." Loretta was a thinly disguised spoof of Dolly herself, and Dolly loved it so much that when Mary Kay Place cut an actual album, *Tonite! At the Capri Lounge: Loretta Haggars*, Dolly Parton sang backup.

RCA had a new album of Dolly's, and they wanted national exposure of the new Dolly. The record company decreed: It was time to go out on the road with her new rocking sound and her rocking band of "glitter gypsies," as she called them, Gypsy Fever, a name she made up herself. "They make me proud of them and proud of myself," said Dolly of her new musicians.

But first, Dolly took a two-week hiatus from work to rest those chronically troubled vocal cords, whose nodes had once more swelled. Her doctor was now the eminent Beverly Hills throat specialist Dr. Edward Kantor, who had operated on Neil Young's nodes. Dr. Kantor ordered total rest of the troubled cords. No singing, no talking for

14 days. Then she would be ready to roll out in her custom-built $180,000 tour bus.

The bus, in which she traveled with "her family," as she called the band, is Dolly's home away from home. It sleeps 11, with a separate little bedroom for Dolly, and comes fully equipped with color TV, a full recording studio with reel-to-reel tape deck and cassette stereo, small kitchen with refrigerator, not one but two bathrooms, a CB radio, and some sizable closets to hold all her shiny costumes and wigs. When, in 1987, Oprah Winfrey asked Dolly Parton how many wigs she owned, Dolly laughed and said, "Lemme see, there are three hundred sixty-five days in a year, and I have a different wig for every day. . . ." But she usually brings no more than 30 or 40 with her for a month-long tour.

In January 1977, Dolly Parton and her backup band of eight men, Gypsy Fever, began a tour of one-night stands in small cities—Battle Creek, Peoria—as a kind of shakedown cruise to get them ready for the big time. Then, aiming at the stars, they went for the big cities—San Francisco, where they played the Boarding House and scored a monster hit with transvestites; the Roxy on Sunset in Los Angeles; the Anaheim Convention Center, where they shared the bill with Mac Davis and opened the show for him, warming up the audience with a 50-minute set by a performer "fresh from a Grammy nomination as Best Country Vocalist," as *Billboard* called Dolly.

Everywhere Dolly Parton and Gypsy Fever played, it was standing room only, with scalpers' prices for the hotly desired tickets. Time magazine reporter Jean Vallely, covering one of the gigs, wrote, "A Dolly Parton concert is a treat, like a hot-fudge sundae after a month of dieting."

Having reached for the stars, Dolly Parton next turned her attention to the moon. "If you can make it there, you'll make it anywhere" is sung only of New York City. The climax of the Gypsy Fever tour was New York's most famous music club, The Bottom Line in Greenwich Village. A small room, but highly selective in its choice of music acts, it is what's called in the business "a showcase." From a successful run at The Bottom Line, many performers have gone on to fill Madison Square Garden.

Dolly was booked into the club for a heavily publicized three-night gig beginning May 13, 1977. Apart from her opening number, Jackie Wilson's famous rhythm-and-blues classic, "Higher and Higher," she performed only her own music, accompanying herself at various times on her guitar, her banjo, and that sweet, sad instrument of Elizabethan ballads, the dulcimer.

*Rolling Stone's* Chet Flippo was among the reporters covering her opening, and he was obviously smitten, pointing out that "Anyone who writes the way she does and sounds like Linda Ronstadt and Emmylou Harris double-tracking themselves and who looks like a triple-dip Baskin-Robbins can probably do no wrong." (Parenthetically, this was hardly the first time that the Parton looks were compared with ice cream. All that pink-and-white-and-golden lusciousness has most often been called "vanilla ice cream." But Dolly

131

herself says, "I don't want to be vanilla. I want to be Rocky Road.")

"The moment she sashayed onstage in a cloud of pink chiffon," rhapsodized Flippo, flipping, "and lit into 'Higher and Higher,' New York City was in the palm of her hand: King Kong with blond hair/wig striding unchecked through lower Manhattan. . . . About the time she started doing only her own material, Parton could have just waved a magic wand right then and there and been done with it, so utterly charmed was her [supposedly] tough New York audience. Hard-bitten Gotham critics were leaping to their feet cheering, and later, at her party atop Kong's World Trade Center, all of them told similar stories to the effect of 'I knew her when.' "

That was quite a party on the night of Dolly Parton's opening, her first engagement in New York City since the disastrous joint concert at the Felt Forum. RCA Records footed the bill for the extravagant party, held at Windows on the World, the class-A restaurant on the 107th floor of the World Trade Center, where, in 1977, every publicity party worth its salty canapés was held.

Dolly played a midnight concert at The Bottom Line. Then the "A" list of invitees was limoed downtown to Windows for a champagne breakfast around 2 A.M. Her performances were packed with celebrities the likes of Mick Jagger, Phoebe Snow, Berry Berenson, Olivia Newton-John, Robert Duvall, who would play a country music singer years later in *Tender Mercies*, Candice Bergen, song stylist Barbara Cook, "Saturday Night Live" star John Belushi, rocker Patti Smith, Bruce

Springsteen at the beginning of his own meteoric rise, and Andy Warhol, who, it was said, would go to the opening of an envelope. They showed up on opening night to cheer the country girl who was crossing over. They were among those who were ready, in Chet Flippo's words, "to crawl right up into her sequined lap and live there happily ever after." Dolly Parton had arrived, and was taking the town by storm with her music.

Her old friend and fan from *The New York Times*, John Rockwell, was also at The Bottom Line on opening night. "It was a triumph," he wrote. "The packed crowd cheered on Miss Parton supportively from the moment she swept onto the stage, and rewarded her with an idolatrous ovation at the end. . . . The band was far better than her old family ensemble had sounded . . . her repertory of self-parodying, sexist jokes was much tamed, very much to the good . . . and her singing sounded finer than ever [she had had a shot of cortisone for her throat troubles]. Miss Parton is blessed with a remarkably individual soprano, nasal and bluegrassy at full volume, and innocently girlish at softer dynamic levels. Her sense of phrasing and pitch are impeccable. Above all, there is her radiant charm, which emerges all the more unencumbered now that she's jettisoned some of her more corny country routines."

Dolly's personal manager at Katz Gallin Cleary was Sandy Gallin. Sandy had wanted Dolly to work with a record producer when she cut her next album, *New Harvest, First Gathering*, but Dolly was determined to produce the album herself. After much discussion, the two arrived at a compromise.

"When Dolly came to me she wanted very badly to write and produce her own material," says Gallin. "She had always been under the auspices of Porter Wagoner, and I felt it was only fair she be given a chance to produce her own album. But we made an agreement that if *New Harvest, First Gathering* wasn't a sales success, or if it didn't produce a hit single, that I could pick an outside producer to do the next album."

Released in the summer of 1977, *New Harvest, First Gathering* was a qualified success when it was released. Dolly was backed up on the album by her new road band, Gypsy Fever. All but two of the songs on the album—"My Love," a reworking of the old Temptations hit "My Girl," and "Higher and Higher"—were written by Dolly, and they included "Getting in My Way" and "Light of a Clear Blue Morning," the only song on the album released as a single, and the song that *Time* magazine called a "declaration of artistic independence."

There was some rock beat and even some disco beat to be heard, but the portrait of Dolly on the album cover, wearing a faded old Levi's jacket and a workman's cap on the back of her wig, went to prove that, be it rock, pop, disco, or country, it was still the same good ole down-home Dolly Parton. Still, it was overproduced and overarranged, neither one thing nor the other.

As stated earlier, the success of the album was qualified. The single went only to number 11 on the country charts, not even into the Top Ten, and reached a dismal number 87 on the pop charts, in the Top One Hundred, but only barely.

The album itself fared somewhat better, number 1 on the country charts, and on the pop charts rising as high as number 38, the highest any album of hers had ever gone on the non-country charts. But it wasn't high enough to suit either Sandy Gallin or Dolly Parton, and she bowed to their previous agreement: Sandy would select a co-producer with professional know-how to guide Dolly's choices, her arrangements, and her work in the studio.

The new record production company was to be Charles Koppelman's The Entertainment Company, and the producer selected by Gallin was Gary Klein, a man of proven creative direction. Klein had been Mac Davis's producer on *Stop and Smell the Roses*, and he had also produced Glen Campbell's *Southern Nights*, which went to number one on the charts, and Barbra Streisand's hit album *Superman*. Dolly Parton's first single with Klein was to become her first mainstream hit.

"Here You Come Again," the upbeat song that was to become a Dolly Parton all-time classic, a song that came to be one of the four or five identified with her, was, oddly enough, not written by Dolly Parton, but by the team of Barry Mann and Cynthia Weil. Also, oddly enough, it wasn't even written *for* her, but had been recorded previously by several other artists, including B. J. Thomas. Released as a single on October 6, 1977, as the title cut for the *Here You Come Again* album, her eleventh solo LP, it went climbing up the pop charts at the same time it went to number one on the country charts.

At first, Dolly didn't want to record the song;

she objected to it as simply too slick and pop. Afraid it would offend her country audience as the wrong material, terrified that her fans would think she was selling out, she told Gallin, "I'm not going to trust you again if the country people don't like this."

But Gary Klein had faith in the song; he felt in his bones, even before the song was mixed, that it would be the breakout crossover single for Dolly Parton. Still, he listened to Dolly's creative suggestions; for example, when she requested that he add a pedal steel guitar, the quintessential country music instrument, to the arrangement, he did so.

"Here You Come Again," the first song Dolly did after she made her changes, was not exactly what she had in mind; she knew it would be a hit, but she wasn't sure it would be a good thing for her to be identified with, because it had such a smooth pop sound. "That's such a good song a monkey could have made it a hit. Well, you're looking at a million-dollar monkey," she laughingly said about it later.

Klein also took Dolly Parton one major step further into the mainstream, cutting the number of original Dolly songs on the *Here You Come Again* album to four, instead of the eight that she had written on *New Harvest, First Gathering*, which included "Applejack," the song she had backed up with so many of her "Grand Ole Opry" pals. The four included "Me and Little Andy," a song she sang in a child's voice, about the death of a child and a pet dog, that is a real tearjerker, and which Dolly still sings in concert; "Cowgirl and the Dandy"; "As Soon as I Touched Him"; and her famous "Two Doors Down."

As soon as the single was released, it was promoted heavily to pop stations. By that time, the publicity blitz set up by Katz Gallin Cleary, the guest appearances on Johnny Carson and other major television shows, the live appearances in clubs that didn't pull in country audiences, had made the pop stations and deejays very aware of the new Miss Dolly Parton, and they gave the cut heavy airplay. Dolly was on her way to the top of the pop charts, just as she had planned to be.

Even the album cover for *Here You Come Again* was designed as a cross between country and pop. Photographed by the eminent album cover camera artist Ed Caraeff in a far more glossy and glamorous way than any of her previous albums, the cover showed not one but *three* laughing, strutting Dollys against a neon background. So much for pop. But the Dollys were dressed country-Dolly style, in skintight jeans rolled up at the cuffs, and a bright red polka-dot blouse tied at the waist. Unmistakably Tennessee. At the same time, Caraeff devised the exuberant signature scrawl of her name, "Dolly," that would be used as a logo on the covers of her other albums.

The combination of Dolly Parton and Gary Klein was a winner; for the first time she had a record producer who was listening to her. For the first time it was a collaborative effort, not Porter Wagoner's "my way," and Dolly's creative instincts and musical input were heard, appreciated, and followed. Under the aegis of Gallin, Koppelman, and Klein, Dolly Parton had a potentially platinum album in *Here You Come Again*, and it did go platinum in early 1980. But in late 1977, it went soaring up the charts, one of the Top Ten in both the pop and the country lists, and was still on the lists through 1978 and into 1979. Her next album with Klein, *Heartbreaker*, went gold. Not only that, but an album she had released back in 1975, *The Best of Dolly Parton*, also went gold, selling more than 500,000 copies, proving that her acceptance as an entertainer, not just a *country* entertainer, was confirmed.

To back up the album, Dolly Parton and Gypsy Fever went on the road again, kicking off their fall tour with a concert in Memphis, and following it the next day with a benefit performance for the Sevier County High School, Dolly's fifth such benefit in seven years. Proceeds from the sold-out concert, which was held in her old high school gymnasium, were donated for uniforms, equipment, and instruments for the high school marching band, Dolly's only happy memory from her own Sevier High years. Sevierville, no longer satisfied with holding a Dolly Parton Day, now proclaimed it Dolly Parton Week.

In October, the Country Music Association held its annual awards presentation, with gala television coverage. Dolly was very much present, although she garnered no awards, probably because there were still bitter feelings that Dolly Parton had deserted country, her protests to the contrary notwithstanding. But a high point of the televised proceedings was the hilarious dialogue between Dolly and Minnie Pearl, proving that not only could Dolly be funny, but that she could still be as down-home as the best of them. There they were, as different-looking as two women can be, Dolly all glamorous in her glitter, with a large jeweled flower in her wig, and Minnie in her trademark "store-bought" hat and calico dress, but sharing the same roots and the same country wisdom and folksy humor.

In December, Dolly arrived in Sacramento, California's state capital, for Dolly Parton Day. She was named Honorary First Lady of Sacramento, and was presented with the keys to the city, the twelfth time within three months that Dolly had been handed keys to a city. Her key ring must have weighed 1,000 pounds; on it were keys to the two Kansas Cities, both in Kansas and Missouri, Wichita Falls, Texas, and St. Louis, among other burgs that had likewise honored her. After a sold-out concert in the Sacramento Memorial Auditorium, Dolly flew back to Los Angeles to appear as Johnny Carson's guest on "The Tonight Show" for the third time that year. In December 1977, she was accorded an outstanding sign of recognition, being chosen as a guest on a Barbara Walters TV special. There, with a sizable block of time at her disposal, she was able to deliver a serious version of her life story along with her many famous wisecracks. There, for the first time, a large audience got to know the real Dolly Parton, the heart underneath the rhinestones and the brain underneath the wigs.

Although she didn't win any awards from the Country Music Association that year, which was most probably due to resentment about the break with Nashville, the move to Los Angeles, and the crossover, Dolly Parton finished 1977 in a state of triumph. Her financial situation had improved dramatically, from the $60,000 a year she had been making with Porter Wagoner, to the $2,500 to $3,000 a night she had been earning with the Travelin' Family Band, to $30,000 for a single engagement. She was now a successful entrepreneur, owning several companies—3 music publishing companies, lots of property, a 23-room mansion in Nashville, other homes, tax shelters by the dozens; she was even about to launch her own film-production company. But she had made much larger strides forward than money alone could measure.

Dolly Parton's crossover had been, on the whole, an immense success—how big, even she couldn't begin to suspect yet. She had held on to her faithful country fans and added millions of new ones. She had proved that she could communicate her thoughts and emotions, as expressed in her songs, to a much wider audience. As a performer, Dolly had evolved naturally, successfully crossing the line, and making "the line," in her case, an imaginary boundary. Now her records were high on both charts. Yet there was more—much more—to come. The fruits of the changes Dolly Parton had made were still to be reaped.

# *Chapter Eight*

## Having It All

I want myself to be happy. I like myself. I'm all I've got. So why can't I have the best for myself?

—Dolly Parton

The impact Dolly Parton made on the field of popular music was felt strongly in 1978, the year Dolly captured three BMI country awards, proof positive that she hadn't lost her country fans while crossing over into mainstream music. Dolly also received important recognition from her peers, the very prestigious Hitmakers Award from the Songwriters Hall of Fame.

Nineteen seventy-eight was also the year when

141

AGVA, the American Guild of Variety Artists, named Dolly Parton Best Female Country Performer of the Year, an honor repeated in 1979.

Nineteen seventy-eight was the year when Dolly Parton won the top honor in the music business, her first Grammy Award, for Best Female Country Vocalist performance on a single, thanks to "Here You Come Again."

But, more important than any of these, 1978 was the year when Dolly was handed what she had always prayed for; in October, at its twelfth annual presentation telecast from Nashville, Dolly Parton was voted not merely Best *Female* Entertainer, but Entertainer of the Year by the Country Music Association, the single highest award that the CMA can bestow. Dolly's cup was overflowing with self-righteous happiness; she could ask for no better confirmation that her hotly disputed career moves had been wise decisions.

It wasn't in Dolly *not* to be outrageous, even when accepting honors. She had been gaining weight steadily ("Everybody loves a fat girl," she joked), but she was still stuffing herself into skin-tight gowns like sausage into a casing. Only minutes before the announcement that Dolly Parton had won Entertainer of the Year, the front of her overfilled custom-made dress split right down the middle, proving that "they" *were* real and "they" *were* all hers, the two questions most frequently asked by interviewers and the public alike.

"Oh, well," said an embarrassed Dolly, grinning. "My daddy always said you shouldn't try to stuff fifty pounds o' mud into a five-pound sack." Only Daddy didn't say *mud*.

"It sure feels great to win when you know you've done your best," said a smiling Dolly, tightly clutching the long-awaited CMA Best Entertainer award. "It's nice to be a winning horse. If I win, I'm always glad. If I lose, well, I just try to work harder the next year."

In 1976, Dolly Parton turned thirty, a traumatic year for any woman. Instead of checking her mirror for crow's feet, Dolly did a reality check on who she was, where she was heading, and, most important, what she wanted out of her life and her career. As usual, she made up one of her "lists." While the nay-sayers protested her change of direction, Dolly had relied as usual upon her own inner strength, and had carefully selected a new "cabinet," a new set of high-powered advisors whose performance in business was well matched to her own.

It had taken her most of two years, 1976 and 1977, to set her career into motion and pick up momentum. But by the end of 1977 a whole new world had opened up to her, a world where Dolly's own assessment of her potential was realized in practical terms—money and fame. Now it was time to maximize that potential to its fullest.

Nineteen seventy-eight and 1979 were big years in Dolly's hot new career, years in which she consolidated her gains and took bold forward steps under the guidance of her new management. *Here You Come Again* was still high on all the charts; her earlier *Best of Dolly Parton* album went gold. By late summer she had two hit singles, "Heartbreaker" and "Baby I'm Burnin' " backed with "I Really Got the Feeling," followed by the *Heart-*

breaker album, which began climbing the charts. Less country than middle of the road, *Heartbreaker* featured a new, lush Dolly Parton with new, lush arrangements, plenty of horns and plenty of strings, arrangements the angry *Rolling Stone* reviewer Tom Carson said "sound like the Longines Symphonette on angel dust." Carson, furious at what he believed to be Parton's MOR sellout, called Dolly "a great American joke—a celeb windup doll."

*Heartbreaker* was followed by *Great Balls of Fire*, which contained the hit singles "Sweet Summer Lovin' " backed by "Great Balls of Fire" and "You're the Only One," neither song written by Dolly. Noel Coppage of *Stereo Review* sneered at the album, saying that it "seems openly to take aim at the Me Decade's sugar/junk fixation, and what it shoots are not great balls of fire, but little balls of bonbons," and sniping at Dolly herself as "a stalker of superstardom." Both albums had the mellow or brassy arrangements that assured them of popular if not critical success, and both did well at the cash registers—*Heartbreaker* went gold in early 1980. *Great Balls of Fire*, which also went gold, contained only four Dolly-written songs (she was composing less since the crossover) —"Sandy's Song," "Down," "Star of the Show," and "Do You Think That Time Stands Still?"

But if some critics turned away in disgust from the new Dolly Parton, she was crying all the way to the bank, and the tears she shed were solid gold. The public adored her. Now, thanks to the magazine covers she adorned and the TV shows she guested on, her mass-media exposure on the

Johnny Carson and Barbara Walters shows, Dolly Parton was instantly recognized, even by the non-musical public. Those wigs and those boobs—they were known everywhere. Drag queens and transvestite performers added Dolly to the catalog of drag acts; she became a great favorite, both live and in cross-dress takeoff, of female impersonators and homosexual enthusiasts. She was delighted by the fervor of her gay fans.

"I have a pretty large gay following, particularly in New York, San Francisco, and Los Angeles," she was quoted. "They're a great audience; they really know how to stir up an entertainer's energy. And I think they like me 'cause I look like fun. They get a kick out of me, especially the guys who dress up in drag. Let me tell ya, it's really somethin' to look out in the audience and see ten or twelve Dolly Partons starin' back at me."

Dolly wasn't one to sit around doing needlepoint. Spending more than a week in the Nashville dream house with Carl the dream husband made Dolly itchy and nervous. She needed to be out there performing. On tour to promote her new albums, she filled houses everywhere she went. Even Down Under in Australia, where she played two concerts in 1979, with the opening act an Australian group called Goldrush, business was SRO. Her personal manager, Sandy Gallin, accompanied Dolly on a "business tour" of Australia, which sent tongues a-waggin' all over again, but Dolly came home to Carl Dean.

In 1978 and 1979, she toured with Eddie Rabbitt

as her opener, even singing duets with him (shades of Porter Wagoner!), but it was as a single that Dolly Parton conquered New York again in the summer of 1978, when she packed the Palladium with wall-to-wall fans and celebrities for two days of concerts.

In New York Dolly did a typically Dolly thing—she gave a free concert, what she called "a people's concert." She even gave a "people's press conference," answering with great good nature the shouted questions, most of which inevitably had to do with those old chestnuts: Were those famous twin assets of hers real, and were they all hers?

"Ah guess they better be, honey," she called out. "Nobody else I know would wanna lay claim to 'em."

Outdoors, on the steps of City Hall, in the bright heat of an August noontime, dressed in a long ruffled chiffon gown with handkerchief hem, Dolly sang to a crowd of 5,000 downtown workers during their lunch hour, and she captured every heart, including Mayor Edward I. Koch's, who doted on show-biz showoff occasions like this one.

"New York," said Dolly after Mayor Koch had presented her with yet another key to yet another city (by then, her key ring must have attained the weight of a small pickup truck), "is the center of the world. I just want to personally thank the people here who have helped me on my way." Then, to wild cheering, she gave them the songs from her *Heartbreaker* album.

Dolly Parton's Palladium concert, played and sung before a crowd of 4,000, took her back to her country-music roots. She sang "Jolene," "Coat of Many Colors," "My Tennessee Mountain Home," "Applejack," "Me and Little Andy," "The Tennessee Waltz," and other down-home favorites. Then she crossed over into "Here You Come Again," "Heartbreaker," and "Two Doors Down." As *Country Music* magazine said, "That night at the Palladium, she could have been a flat-chested brunette in army fatigues and it would have made no difference."

*Time* magazine described Dolly as "looking like a purple Popsicle (dragging out that old ice-cream image one more time) in a gown designed to accentuate more curves than a good knuckle ball."

Dolly's major triumph after New York was playing the Universal Amphitheater in Los Angeles, an auditorium so large that "I never wanted to play there until I thought I could draw a big crowd." Even with the monster house entirely sold out, "It's fillin' me with tension, because I know there will be a lot of music and film people and a lot of writers and critics in the audience."

Dolly needn't have worried her pretty little platinum wig; the series of concerts—September 21–24, 1979—played brilliantly.

But Dolly couldn't stay on the road forever. Sooner or later, she had to come home to Carl.

Five years earlier, Dolly and Carl had built their dream house, from the ground up, an antebellum Southern mansion on a fenced-in hill about 5 miles outside Nashville, surrounded by 200 acres of lush farmland. In October 1973, in his interview in *Country Music* magazine, Dolly had told Jerry Bailey, "We're going to raise whiteface cattle when we get our own farm. We've just got about ten acres now, but we're waiting until we can get into our new house, which will be in early spring. It's out in the Brentwood area, in the farm section. Out there, there's about seventy acres, and we have another farm out near Franklin. That's where we have our cattle and pigs and everything.

"When we get our house, we're going to move the animals we want around us out there. We've got half our house done; it's a Southern plantation house. In fact, we're going to call it Willow Lake Plantation. We have a lake with a lot of willow trees planted around it.

"It's a real big house—one I always dreamed about. I don't have many rooms, but the rooms I have are real big and I have a real big living room and dining room and a long kitchen. In fact, I'm going to have two kitchens in one. One end will have the modern conveniences I really need, and the other will have an old wooden stove that really works. In the wintertime, sometimes, I'm going to use it."

The finished house was not much different from Dolly's rhapsodic description, although the "not many" rooms turned out to be 23, which translates into "many" in anybody's vocabulary. But they needed the room, because of Dolly's large family. Dolly and Carl took on the job of raising her five youngest brothers and sisters at Tara, which was what they called the six-pillared home with its deep verandas on the upper and lower stories, because it was modeled closely after Scarlett O'Hara's plantation in *Gone With the*

*Wind*. With no children of her own, Dolly expended her maternal energies on her kid brothers and sisters, as she would later on her many nieces and nephews.

She needed the room, too, for her "working clothes," 12 walk-in closets packed with rhinestoned and sequined outfits, a reported 3,000 of them, not to mention the many, many pairs of 5-inch-heeled shoes, and storage for a couple of hundred very expensive wigs. "You'd never believe," Dolly would quip to her Las Vegas audiences, "how danged expensive it is to look this cheap."

At one point, Dolly moved her parents, Avie Lee and Robert Lee, to a large house in Nashville to be near her, but they hated being in the city, so she bought them a farm with a large, comfortable house, near Sevierville, and they gratefully moved back home.

But Dolly doesn't let go of her kinfolk that readily. Most of her close relatives live close by Tara, and Dolly and Carl keep a mobile home at the big house to accommodate her mama and daddy when they visit. Dolly and Carl raise whiteface Hereford cattle, as well as a couple of bloodhounds and a pair of peacocks. Because, as Dolly says, her own taste runs so much to the gaudy, she called in professional decorators to embellish her home—in fact, all her homes. But there were many finishing touches in it that were Dolly's and Carl's own, such as the wooden facing for the living room fireplace, made of logs taken from the original Pigeon River cabin in which Dolly had been born. The logs were salvaged when the cabin was being torn down. The house is set well back from the road, and is fenced in for complete privacy, with tall gates in front of the long driveway.

However, in 1976 Dolly Parton had told Chris Chase of *The New York Times* that, while the house was beautiful, she didn't know "if I'm enjoyin' it or not. It just bothers my mind to feel that I have so much and that so many have so little," and, although, as Chase added, that Dolly couldn't "bring herself to put in a swimming pool ("That's one of them things like a five-hundred-dollar coat; I keep thinkin' there's something else I can do besides build a pool")," Dolly and Carl did in fact wind up with a swimming pool (and Dolly with at least a $500 coat). Not only a pool, but a hot tub, and all this in addition to the creek that runs through the property and the small picturesque private lake surrounded by willow trees that gives the estate its name of Willow Lake Plantation. As for Dolly Parton having "so much," she wanted more. And she got it.

Mr. and Mrs. Carl Dean enjoy the good life on the farm, whenever Dolly isn't in Los Angeles or New York or on the road or in the studio. They have so many visitors that "the house is like a hotel," jokes Dolly. "We got a register book and we even put up some credit card stickers on the door." But the visitors are all private—family and friends, people with whom Carl Dean feels comfortable. No business associates are allowed at Tara; Dolly keeps a place in Los Angeles for that, another in New York, and a third in Nashville.

In 1979, Dolly Parton added several new dimensions to her professional life. She opened an office in New York City, which is actually a modern art-filled, decorator-adorned apartment on the twenty-sixth floor, high above Fifth Avenue, which she shares, a few days a month, with her personal manager, Sandy Gallin. Naturally, there was gossip about the two, the same kind of gossip that surrounded Dolly and Porter Wagoner, and, just as naturally, Dolly denied it. The apartment was strictly for business, she said. Parton and Gallin were forming a new music company of their own, together with RCA Records and Gallin's partner Raymond Katz of Katz Gallin Cleary.

The name of the new company was White Diamond Records, to be distributed by RCA, and based in the Katz Gallin Cleary offices in Beverly Hills. They aimed to have a new Dolly Parton album out by the time Dolly made her first Las Vegas appearance at the Riviera Hotel.

The apartment was decorated and furnished in cool whites and neutrals by designer Barbara Rosen, and adorned with costly artworks that Gallin collects, such as two Claes Oldenburg paintings and one by Robert Rauschenberg. Dolly ignores them, although she collects paintings herself; hers are by Ben Hampton, whose Tennessee scenes remind her of Norman Rockwell. Dolly Parton may not know much about art, but she knows what she likes.

"When I see a picture I like, I buy it, whether it costs a lot or a little," she told Georgia Dullea of The New York Times. "But I have to be honest and tell you some of the pictures in this apartment cost a lot and I can't help thinkin', 'Good

Lord, I coulda done that in first grade. Guess that just goes to show you I ain't got no taste.' "

In October 1979, country music came to the White House. The President, Jimmy Carter, was a good ole boy from Georgia, and he proclaimed October as Country Music Month, perhaps because of a televised country music concert to be played October 2 in Washington, D.C. Carter, who went to the concert, invited country favorites Johnny Cash, June Carter, The Oak Ridge Boys, Ronnie Milsap, Bill Monroe, Tom T. Hall, the Bluegrass Boys, Glen Campbell, Dottie West, and others to lunch at the White House. President Jimmy went down the reception line shaking hands with everybody until he came to Dolly Parton.

"You're the one I've been waiting for," he said, grinning that famous toothy grin and grabbing her for a hug.

"Get a good one now." Dolly grinned back. Presidents or big-rig drivers, it was all the same to her. Dolly Parton loved them all, and they loved her back.

Also, toward the end of 1979, after holding out for years while her price increased astronomically, Dolly Parton signed a multimillion-dollar agreement to play Las Vegas, another long-held ambition of hers, no matter how often she'd denied it publicly.

"I got to the point where I could have a big deal in Vegas, but I didn't want to work Vegas until I could go there as myself with good music, until I could have the power to draw people, and also have enough power to say what kinda show I would do."

Vegas was where the big money was to be found, not to mention the boost such an engagement would give her record sales. The contract called for Dolly to play the Riviera Hotel, six weeks a year, from 1980 through 1982, and the sums involved made Dolly one of the richest female entertainers in the world. The amounts most commonly mentioned varied between $6,000,000 and $9,000,000, the highest price ever paid to a Vegas entertainer, which for an 18-week contract breaks down to $350,000 to $500,000 a week! All this for a girl who had started her singing career at $20 a week! What a way to bring a decade of change to an end!

The "holdback" Dolly Parton felt within her was gone now. "I really don't know anythin' but what comes out of my own heart. I'm happier now than ever before, bein' more my own person, goin' in new directions."

Dolly Parton had everything an Entertainer of the Year could possibly want—money, tax shelters, honors and awards, fans, a platinum album, royalties from records and songs, all of them tangible proof that she'd made the right moves and the correct career decisions; a high visibility quotient—she was so recognizable, so much larger than life. Drag shows throughout the country had added Dolly Parton segments to their lip-synch performances, and straight as well as gay Dolly Parton Lookalike contests were held somewhere in America in any week one would care to name. When shown photographs of the contestants, Dolly usually selected the male entries as better-looking and more "real" than the females!

Dolly Parton now had fame and fortune.

She owned property, houses, apartments, and stores. She was occasionally living in her dream house, the one she had always wanted, designed and built entirely to her own specifications. She had an apartment in Los Angeles, one on Fifth Avenue in New York, offices, corporations, copyrights, cars, youth, beauty, health. She had the satisfaction of knowing she was taking good care of her mama and daddy, and her sisters and brothers. She had a husband she loved and who loved her, who didn't keep her chained, but gave her instead as much freedom as she needed to fly like an eagle.

Dolly Parton had a $9,000,000 Las Vegas contract for only 18 weeks of work a year.

Dolly Parton had a platinum record and a den whose walls were filled with plaques, awards, scrolls, keys to the cities of America, silver and gold cups, and pictures of herself with the President of the United States and with Queen Elizabeth and Prince Philip.

Dolly Parton had everything—except . . .

Dolly Parton wanted to make a movie. She wanted to conquer Hollywood in the same way she had conquered Nashville and later New York and the rest of the country. Without a hit film, one really couldn't call oneself a superstar. Look at Barbra Streisand. A great voice, but it wasn't until she had a few box-office smashes behind her—most notably *Funny Girl*, *The Way We Were*, and *A Star is Born*—that she was admitted into the permanent pantheon of the greats. A hit picture—that's what Miss Dolly was hankering for, and it didn't even have to be a musical.

In 1978, this most recent of Dolly's dreams began to come true. Twentieth Century-Fox signed her to a 3-picture contract. Was Dolly Parton going to be the new Mae West? The new Marilyn Monroe? She had already been approached with tentative plans for vehicles about both legendary sex goddesses, and had turned both projects down flat.

"I'll just be unique," she protested. "I don't like to be compared to anyone, not Marilyn Monroe, not Mae West, either. I'm just gonna be myself, movies or no movies. I'm gonna play Dolly Parton, or at least a Dolly Parton-type character." She also denied she was planning to take acting lessons before breaking into pictures.

But what was the first picture to be? How would Dolly be handled in her film debut? Would she become a movie star overnight, or fall flat on her plump round keister? Dolly Parton was no ordinary property, and this could be no ordinary film. Dolly was thinking hard, and so were her managers, Katz Gallin Cleary. The important thing was not to push her in the water before she could swim, not to launch Dolly Parton into films before she was ready, and then see to it that it was a strong script, the proper vehicle, and a good showcase for her talents. This is not as easy to do as it sounds, and Dolly had been turning down poor or tasteless scripts with some regularity.

Meanwhile, in Los Angeles, Jane Fonda was driving down the Santa Monica Freeway, listening to a new hit song on her car stereo and thinking very, very hard. The song was "Here You Come Again," and what Fonda was thinking about was a film she had decided to produce herself, a film that would be made by her own company, IPC Films, and released by Fox, a clever feminist message-comedy called *Nine to Five*. And she was also thinking hard about a gutsy, busty singer named Dolly Parton.

# *Chapter Nine*

## Working Nine to Five

> I don't even understand that women's liberation stuff, don't know what it's about. I'm a lucky person. I'm liberated, free-spirited, free-minded, but it's not something I promote or push—just a natural way I've always lived.
>
> —Dolly Parton

The first murmurs about *Nine to Five* began to be heard in the late summer of 1979; the film was tentatively scheduled to begin shooting sometime in November, but there wasn't yet a final script. The concept sounded amusing—a comedy about secretaries who get even with their chauvinist boss, and the leads, Jane Fonda, Lily Tomlin, and Dolly Parton, were a riot of a combination, enough to amuse even the most hardened moviegoer.

Here's Fonda, a serious-minded political activist (and fitness nut), and Tomlin, a serious-minded standup comic, two feminist figures teaming up with a feminine figure like fluffy Dolly to make a feminist comedy about exploited women who get their revenge.

From its concept, Jane Fonda, who had a business interest in the film, wanted Lily Tomlin and Dolly Parton to co-star; she was quoted as saying that, when she saw Dolly's photograph on an album cover, she thought to herself, *Boy, does she ever look like everybody's idea of a secretary.*

In a far more serious vein, Jane told Chet Flippo of *Rolling Stone* that, once the decision had been made to make a movie about secretaries, she knew immediately that Dolly should be in it. "I had never met her, but I was really into her music. Anyone who can write 'Coat of Many Colors' and sing it the way she does has got the stuff to do anything. This was not a woman who was a stereotype of a dumb blonde. I felt that she could probably do just about anything she wanted, that this was a very smart woman. We developed a character based on who she is and what she seems like. Did we coach her? No. Her persona is so strong, you get somebody mucking about with that and making her self-conscious, and it could be negative. Even though we're from different backgrounds and different classes, we're very very alike in many ways. Dolly's not political, but her heart, her instincts—she's on the side of the angels. Very often someone will wow you, but as you get to know them, the mystery wears off. One of the things that just flabbergasts me about Dolly is the amount of mystery she has. She's a very mysterious person."

*Nine to Five* wasn't the first movie Dolly Parton had been offered; but it was the first one she accepted. "I didn't say yes until I saw the script," said a savvy Dolly. "If it was only gonna be a buncha boob jokes, I wasn't interested." Even the first-draft version of the *Nine to Five* script intrigued her.

She had been very picky going over scripts. "I hadn't found a script I thought was good enough. I was amazed at how little talent there is among the writers of Hollywood. But *Nine to Five* fascinated me, and I knew instantly that I should do it. I felt it in my heart it was a career move."

"I'm anxious and excited about doing it," she told syndicated movie-biz columnist Marilyn Beck in early September 1979, "but I won't be doing it unless I can do it right—unless I feel I can do my part well. And I won't know that until I've seen the latest rewrite, and then work on it with the writers." Even in her first film, Dolly Parton was already insisting on a measure of artistic control.

"All of us [Tomlin, Fonda, and Parton] have to approve our characters, to make sure they're right for us. And the script, which has already gone through several rewrites, is just now beginning to blossom into the kind of thing that's good—well, at least comin' closer to being good."

Dolly needn't have worried. The part of Doralee Rhodes, the boss's voluptuous secretary in *Nine* to Five, was custom-written for her by Patricia Resnik and Colin Higgins, tailored specifically to suit her personality. Dolly wasn't 100 percent won over by it; after the film opened, she said, "The Doralee role in *Nine to Five* wasn't so great, but she was okay for Dolly's first Hollywood movie role. She could kinda sneak in as a little old fat secretary, cute and lovable and fun." She also commented, "There were places I thought I was real good, but there were also places I was real average and places where I was yuck."

Doralee, with her platinum hair and her tight clothes wrapped around her hourglass figure, is at first a figure of scorn and derision. Because her slavering boss (played brilliantly by Dabney Coleman) so obviously lusts after her, the entire office is certain that she's sleeping with him and that she's nothing but a brassy, cheap-looking bimbo. Actually, she is a hard-working, intelligent young woman, very much in love with and faithful to her husband, who cannot understand why a friendly Southern gal like herself can't make friends with the other women in the office, or why everybody treats her so coldly.

"I'd say that eighty percent of all bosses would make a pass at their secretary, given the chance," commented Dolly, speaking of her role as soon as the producers had the final script in hand. "Sure the boss would try to come on to Doralee; that's human nature. But as the movie goes on, they certainly don't play me as some dumb blonde. Doralee is an intelligent, caring person.

"The film appealed to me because it felt so right. It's a comedy, which I thought I could carry off much better than something heavier. But also, the character was always going to be pretty much the same way as I am. Doralee pretty much has my own personality, so I didn't feel I was going to be just thrown into something real difficult first time out. In the movie, I look like myself. I wear the kind of clothes I usually do wear, like sweaters and tight skirts. I like to dress pretty, and so does Doralee. I don't see her as sexy. I think she's kind of cuddly.

"I don't see myself the way that some people might. I don't think that I look particularly sexy. I had created this image that I liked. You know, the big hair and the costumes. I had been looking the same way since I was about sixteen, and I liked it, so I made it my look. I like to be outrageous, because my personality is so outgoing. And, anyhow, it's worked real well."

For Dolly, *Nine to Five* was a "blessed thing," a "real special project." She said that she "did not have one bad moment on the whole picture."

From a practical point of view, she had chosen well. Her first picture was not a film she would have to carry herself. Starring with such experienced actresses and formidable talents as Lily Tomlin (who had starred in *Nashville*, for which Tomlin had been nominated for an Oscar, and in *The Late Show*) and Jane Fonda (fresh from a personal triumph and an Oscar for *Coming Home*) took a lot of the burden off Dolly's own shoulders. If the film should go floppo and belly-up, Dolly Parton wouldn't be held totally responsible. If, on the other hand, the movie *did* make it at the box office, there was a good chance of Dolly's getting a cut of that success.

Then, too, there was always Dolly's way of looking at the positive side of things, and her optimistic nature. "I was never really afraid. Once I'd said yes to the contract and committed myself to making movies, I knew I'd find a way to make it all work out. I'm a very positive thinker, always have been. I never could find it in myself that I'd fail, and that's why I succeed." If Dolly felt any misgivings about exposing her inexperienced acting (she had never taken an acting lesson) side by side with the proven skills of Tomlin and Fonda, she kept those reservations to herself.

Even so, as something of an insurance policy, Dolly sat down and turned out the film's theme song, a bouncy little number also titled "Nine to Five," which she would sing over the opening credits. If the film bombed, she could always go back to singing. Little did she know.

That Hollywood had opened its doors to the budding actress was made evident when the Motion Picture Academy asked Dolly to be an Oscar presenter in the 1980 Academy Awards ceremonies. Dolly turned up in a skintight dress cut all the way down to "there," causing gasps of shock and delight. But this time, alas, it stayed in one piece.

Although Dolly has always denied that she is a sex symbol, others have not been so unrealistic. In the fall of 1980, Dolly Parton journeyed to Nashville to kick off a special campaign to lure tourists to the state of Tennessee. "If they won't follow Dolly Parton to Tennessee, they won't follow anyone," declared the state governor, Lamar Alexander, as Dolly's 7-foot-high image was plastered on the sides of about 30 18-wheelers carrying the slogan DOLLY DOLLY DOLLY: FOLLOW ME TO TENNESSEE. At a Nashville truck stop, Dolly sloshed champagne over the lead rig, and the campaign was launched. Did Dolly Parton see into the future some 6 years, to a time when she would be making personal millions out of Tennessee tourism?

"I'd never seen a movie being made before," admitted Dolly when *Nine to Five* was wrapped. "I was so silly. I thought that movies were just done as the script goes. So I memorized the whole thing, my part and everyone else's. I knew the whole movie word for word before I ever came out here [Hollywood], which I found hilarious once I saw how movies were made—out of sequence and everything. You open a door one week, and you walk into the room three weeks later.

"But then I found that I didn't have to study so hard during the making of the movie, and making movies is a lot like recording an album, because you go back and do the same things over and over again. Jane has been so helpful about camera angles and lots of technical things, and Lily has been a great inspiration to me. Lily and me, the two of us have a great communication thing going between us, and I get such a big kick out of her."

*Nine to Five* was certainly a comedy, but Jane Fonda also conceived of it as a film with a very definite message—that women are frequently discriminated against in the workplace, receiving less money, less responsibility, and less recognition than their male counterparts.

"Office workers are the power force of the eighties," said Fonda, who had had the idea for a movie about secretaries for 3 years, and had been speaking to office workers' groups as part of her political activism. A number of the groups were called "Nine to Five," the inspiration for the film's title. Cleveland's Working Women, the national association of office workers, gets a line in the movie's credits.

"Y'know," Jane Fonda told writer Cliff Jahr, "I'm not going to spend a whole year of my life making a movie that doesn't raise consciousness, and it is *unbelievable* what's happening. "One group I spoke to in Milwaukee—the clerical workers couldn't use the elevators; they had to walk up the back stairs. Only male executives had a key to the front door. Women were followed to the john, even monitored when they went to lunch. The office structure also pits women against each other very viciously: older women versus young, black and brown versus white, pretty versus ugly, thin versus fat. It's important who dresses better than whom. The sexual tensions, the pay problems, the lack of promotion . . ." Fonda's indignation would be captured by the film.

Budgeted at $10,000,000, *Nine to Five* was also a blatant commercial for Sisterhood Is Powerful. All the women in the film are smart and funny and capable (with the exception of the butt-kissing company fink who is in love with Dabney Coleman), while none of the men in the movie is worth what it costs to dress him. The possible exception is Dolly's handsome truck-driving husband, but he is little more than a beefcake prop.

In a large corporation run by men, where the hard work is done almost entirely by poorly rewarded women, three women work for Dabney Coleman. Fonda's role is Judy Bernly, a recently divorced, timid, and insecure housewife of forty-one, forced, for economic reasons, to take her first job in an office after years of staying at home and being supported by her husband.

Tomlin plays Violet Newstead, the super-efficient and very intelligent office manager (a lower position than it sounds) whose good ideas are always swiped by the boss and passed off as his own, and Dolly is cast as the blond, bubbly personal secretary after whom Coleman, in his role as Franklin Hart, Jr., a braggart tyrant and weenie, lusts in vain, although the liar has boasted to every man in the company that he has already enjoyed her ample charms.

The three women are leery of one another, but one evening, after a particularly trying day for all of them, they bump into one another in a bar, have a few drinks together, and Lily Tomlin and Jane Fonda discover that Doralee isn't sleeping with the boss at all, and isn't teacher's pet or the company fink, but instead stands on the side of the workers.

They wander back to Tomlin's house, where they get high on some grass she scores from her teen-age son. Giggly and stoned on pot, and becoming firm friends, the three women fantasize about getting even with Coleman. Jane Fonda's fantasy is the goriest—dressed like a Great White Hunter, she tracks him through the maze of offices as though he were a wild beast. Then she wastes him with an elephant gun. In Lily Tomlin's fantasy, she is dressed like Snow White, complete with animated Disney bluebirds twittering overhead. She poisons him with a magical potion, then shoves him out a high window.

In Dolly Parton's fantasy, she is a rootin'-tootin' cowgirl, dressed in boots, fringe, Stetson hat, with a gun. In a complete role reversal, *Doralee* is the boss, and the boss is her secretary. Now she turns the tables on Coleman, becoming overtly sexually aggressive, and subjects him to the identical sexual harassment with which he's been torturing her. "Hey, hot stuff!" she yells at him. "Grab a pad and pencil and bring your buns in here!"

Deliberately, Dolly drops the container of pencils off her desk, making her "secretary" go down on his hands and knees to find them, so that she can leer at his behind, just as he has done to sneak a peek into her cleavage. She calls him "cutie," and "sweetheart," and presents him with a necktie he doesn't want, just as he has gifted her with a scarf and forced her to accept and wear it. She ropes and ties him, like the bull that he is. Of all the fantasies in the film, Dolly's is the most lighthearted.

Naturally, the pot-smoking scene was controversial, but, as Dolly explained, "We were just three women trying it once. It's not like we do it all the time. I don't take drugs myself; I don't have to rely on anything like that, not when I've got my music, my family, and the Lord for solace."

Through a farcical series of events, the three women actually manage to kidnap Coleman and keep him locked up in an empty house, then proceed to run the company themselves, doing a bang-up job, of course. They make many changes, and all of them for the better—shared jobs, so that two women can each work part-time; a day-care center for nursery children; and, of course, raises and promotions for the underpaid, over-worked female employees. Despite all their radical moves, business improves. *Nine to Five* ends with all three of them getting promoted, making decent money, and gaining recognition.

The women improve, too. Fonda loses her timidity and gains a new feeling of self-respect and independence as she earns her own living. Tomlin's overly critical character unbends and softens as she achieves solidarity with her fellow workers and earns her long-overdue promotion. The only one who doesn't change is Doralee-Dolly, who was pretty damned perfect to begin with. But at the finish Dolly's situation in the office has been completely reversed—her value and abilities are recognized and applauded, while her bimbo reputation is exposed as a pack of lies. It was an auspicious film debut, especially for an entertainer with no previous acting experience who had been known only as a singer-songwriter.

Journalist Lawrence Grobel, who had interviewed Dolly for *Playboy*, now interviewed her for *Playgirl*, as the publicity wagons for *Nine to*

Five began to roll. "Who did you feel closer to during the filming, Jane or Lily?" he asked her.

"Actually," answered Dolly, "I felt a bit closer to Lily because I had a chance to get to know her, and Jane had so much business stuff to do. Lily and I are both with the same agency now. I spent more time talking to Lily. With Jane, we got to be close, but we really hadn't gotten together enough to totally relax and be just pals. I have such admiration for Jane. I'm not starstruck, but I know when a person's great."

There had been a lot of industry snickering in advance of the filming, as Hollywood pundits tried to imagine Dolly, Lily, and Jane working together. There were jokes about the size of their egos, about their different kinds of bodies, about their different mind-sets. Fonda's radical-style politics are a matter of public record, while, to Dolly, politics are something one never discusses. She won't tell you what they are, but you can bet dollars to greasy doughnuts that a country music gal from the South hasn't the same outlook on the state of the world as an actress who has hit the Chou En Lai trail and visited Hanoi.

"A lot of people were sayin', 'Boy, I would l-o-o-o-ve to see that,' " Dolly said laughingly to Chet Flippo. " 'There ain't no way them three bitches are gonna get along. Can you imagine three women like that?!' And you know, we had the greatest time."

Actually, the pundits were way off base. From day one there was mutual respect, mutual admiration, and a mutual-support group among the three stars on the set of *Nine to Five*. They went out of their way to be good to one another, as if to throw the rumors of potential temperament clashes back into the teeth of the rumor mongers. They drank champagne together, cooked spaghetti, and traded gossip in a sisterly love fest. Shooting the picture was like one big sleepover. The three women did everything but get out their high school yearbooks and give one another Toni home permanents, and maybe they did that, too.

It goes without saying that, during the 9 weeks of filming, Dolly Parton and Jane Fonda did *not* discuss politics. No doubt they didn't discuss workouts, either, since Dolly has often told her public how much she hates to exercise, and that what she really likes is to watch exercise videos like Jane Fonda's workout tapes while sitting still and stuffing her face with greasy, fattening foods.

"She's so nice. She's cotton candy," says Jane of Dolly.

"I'd always loved Lily, but I wondered about me and Jane. Jane comes across hard at times, but she's so much sweeter and softer. She's almost like a little girl," says Dolly of Jane.

But why shouldn't they have gotten along like sisters? If one puts aside their surface differences and examines their similarities, Dolly, Lily, and Jane would be seen to have many characteristics in common. All three are highly intelligent businesswomen who run their own business ventures. All three are hardworking and dedicated to that work. All three are innovative performers, each with a style very much her own. And, bottom line, all three are consummate professionals. Even the non-actress Dolly knew instinctively from the outset of filming how and when to give a scene her all. Her stage sense and presence, her many years of experience before audiences of all types, has made her nearly as much of an actress as a singer.

Of course, there was a lot of technical information and nuances Dolly had to learn about making films. When one is larger than life on the stage, as Dolly is, it has to be toned down for the camera, which is subtle and catches everything. Jane Fonda taught her a number of the professional tricks of the trade, telling Dolly how to look, or turn, or the right way to pause.

"She was always sayin' little things like 'Don't talk on the same voice level.' 'Don't get too excited when you've got nowhere to go.' 'Don't start out high.' 'Make a definite look . . . don't move your eyes around.' Things like that. She also suggested that as a part of my contracts in the future, I might want a coach on the job with me. And she gave me names of directors to think about. A lot of people think she's hard because of her strong beliefs, but I found her very sensitive. She's very firm, very intelligent. She said to me, 'I'd like to see you someday do something really serious and dramatic. Not comedy, not funny.' "

*Nine to Five* opened in 1980 as a Christmas release and was an immediate box-office smash. *Variety* said, "The bottom line is that this picture is a lot of fun. Fonda, Tomlin, and Parton provide charm and distinction to their sketchy characters. . . ." In summation, the trade paper opined, ". . . will get paid handsomely for overtime at the box office." *Variety* was right on target.

Before her first film wrapped, the announcement hit the media that Dolly's second picture would be *The Best Little Whorehouse in Texas* with Burt Reynolds. Dolly Parton had been spoiled by the "blessed thing" that was *Nine to Five*. Her next picture would be a totally different story.

# Chapter Ten

## Dolly on a Roll

A star, you know, is something bright. Something that stands out, that's special. Something *shining*.

—Dolly Parton

The success of the picture *Nine to Five* didn't take many people by surprise. The combination of Parton, Fonda, and Tomlin would make even the merely curious line up for tickets. But what knocked everybody out was the meteoric, phenomenal success of the title song. "Nine to Five," an upbeat country number delivered in Dolly Parton's unmistakable style, swept the nation, soaring up the charts with the speed of an eagle, reaching number one in both the country and the pop markets. Both the single and the album, *Nine to Five and Odd Jobs,* went platinum.

More than that, the song "Nine to Five" became a kind of anthem for working women everywhere, a theme song that expressed their frustrations with "all takin' and no givin'." "I knew that I could write a song about myself and my daddy and my brothers and my sisters and my friends and all the people who work nine to five. 'Workin' nine to five, what a way to make a livin'.'

"I've been tryin' all these years to win my musical freedom so I could introduce myself to another audience, a more universal audience," Dolly had said more than once.

With *Nine to Five,* Dolly Parton had achieved at last that true universality—not everybody grows up poor in Tennessee, but all women work, whether in an office, a factory, the home, or even on a Las Vegas stage. From the launching of the song, there was talk of a Grammy, maybe even an Oscar. When the time came, "Nine to Five" would win two Grammys—as Best Country Song, and for Dolly, as Best Female Country Vocal Performance. It won the 1981 People's Choice Award and was nominated for an Oscar, losing to "Arthur's Theme (Best That You Can Do)" from *Arthur.*

Dolly wrote "Nine to Five" on the set. The only thing that made her itchy about making movies was "hurry up and wait," those endlessly long breaks between scenes, the mindless tedium of the process in which one stands around doing nothing for hours at a time. Dolly Parton is not a nothing-doer, so she filled the idle hours on the set writing songs. She was more creative while making *Nine to Five* than she had been in a good long while.

"The hardest thing was the long wait between shots," she told writer Kip Kirby, "the hours you'd sit in makeup and costume and all. And I thought to myself, now I am not gonna sit around here like this. 'Cause it was the first time in my life that I've ever had to sit around and do nothin'. I can't embroider or nothin' like that, so I figured if I started writin' songs, it would change my mood. So I started writin' right on the set, and I was amazed at how easily I could do it. That's how I wrote 'Nine to Five.' "

After the film was wrapped, Dolly and Jane Fonda took a trip together down South. Jane's next project was to be a TV movie, "The Doll-maker," based on the prize-winning novel by Harriet S. Arnow; it would win a well-deserved Emmy for Fonda. Set in the Appalachian Mountains, it's the story of a mountain woman, dirt-poor, with the miraculous skill of hand-carving folk-art dolls, and Jane went south to research it, taking the mountain woman Dolly Parton with her.

"We traveled around together for a week," Dolly told Lawrence Grobel. "We just had the best time you could imagine. We totally relaxed. It was like I was a little girl having a great time in the country entertaining a city cousin. In fact, we came up with some great ideas for movies and series and stories. It was really special. It was hard to say good-bye. We became good friends."

*Nine to Five* was a favorite with the press and the critics, as well as the public. It became one of the smash hits of 1980–1981. The lion's share of the publicity on the picture went to Dolly Parton, who not only made an excellent film debut as Doralee, but had written the title song and a number of others on the soundtrack album.

*Nine to Five and Odd Jobs* was the title of the album. It was a concept album about working people, just as *My Tennessee Mountain Home* was a concept album about Dolly's days of struggle before her success. It included a Merle Travis classic about coal mining, "Dark as a Dungeon," a Woody Guthrie classic, "Deportee (Train Wreck at Los Gatos)," and "The House of the Rising Sun," a low-down blues about girls who are ruined in a New Orleans bordello. "Hush-a-Bye Hard Times" was written by Dolly in the bluegrass mode; another Dolly Parton original was "Working Girl."

*Nine to Five* wasn't the only Dolly Parton album RCA released in 1980—she'd also done *Dolly Dolly Dolly* and *Heartbreak Express*. Of *Dolly Dolly Dolly*, Kelly Delaney wrote in *Country Music* magazine that the album was "like a brand-new car— polished to a fine glaze with chrome shining brilliantly. . . . Much of the album is like mindless car radio music which fits nicely between jockey chatter, traffic reports, and the latest afternoon racing results. With few exceptions, there are no memorable music or lyrics. . . . *Dolly Dolly Dolly* is only so much folly folly folly."

But it was a much different story with *Nine to Five and Odd Jobs*. In October 1981, the title song won the BMI Robert J. Burton Award for the Country Song of the Year. It was also on BMI's published list of "Most Performed Hits" for 1981, and the listing carried a star, meaning that it had passed 1,000,000 performances. Dolly was on the program of the 1981 Academy Awards telecast, where, dressed in sequins, she sang the nominated "Nine to Five," which received an ovation, even though it didn't win.

Record reviewers fell all over themselves to praise the *Nine to Five* album. Stephen Holden, who had dismissed the Dolly Parton of *Dolly Dolly Dolly* as sounding "like a windup toy," said of *Nine to Five*, "After a string of abysmal pop records on which her kittenish treatment of fatuous material turned her into a bad joke, Dolly Parton makes an impressive comeback with *Nine to Five and Odd Jobs*." Holden concluded his review: "It's nice to have Dolly Parton back from the trash bin unscathed."

Bob Campbell of *Country Music* magazine said that *Nine to Five and Odd Jobs* "is more varied and down to earth than what we have heard from Dolly in some time, and she gives us our money's worth. But I suspect her next album will be the real killer."

It was.

Between *New Harvest, First Gathering* and *Nine to Five and Odd Jobs*, Dolly Parton had recorded a series of Gary Klein-produced albums at Hollywood's Sound Lab studios. They were popular, they were well-put-together, and featured heavy-beat, full-instrumentation arrangements. Even though they all made the charts, they showed a side of Dolly that was offensive to country purists. A number of the songs were "country-flavored," but none of them was country music as the old Dolly Parton could do country music.

Probably nobody was more aware of that problem than Dolly herself, because Parton went back to Nashville to record *Nine to Five and Odd Jobs,* her first album to be cut in Music City, U.S.A., since *New Harvest, First Gathering.* The sound she was looking for, she said, was a sound that lived in Nashville.

The "return" to Nashville was a triumph, as Dolly revealed her plans to open her own company on Music Row (as though she didn't have heavy business interests there already, with companies like Owepar Publishing). But this new venture, by means of which, Dolly announced, she would put "back into Nashville some of the things I learned since I started out," was to be a highpowered, multilevel organization that would combine management, booking, recording, and song publishing, not only for Dolly Parton herself but for other artists. She also promised to build a recording studio in Nashville, and she made a vow that her next album after *Nine to Five and Odd Jobs* would be pure country, all her own songs.

This announcement of the new company "coincided" with the Nashville premiere of *Nine to Five,* which included, in addition to all the hoopla that attends such a media event—the press conferences, the photographs of celebrities on the front pages of the local papers, and the interviews on radio and TV—a gala invitation-only screening of the motion picture, plus a big party afterward, for the top-drawer crowd of country music and record executives.

Since Dolly Parton and Porter Wagoner had finally settled their dragged-out lawsuit out of court, Dolly tried to bury the hatchet by inviting Porter to the premiere of the film. Wagoner didn't show up, and the two of them were not to get together publicly until the sixtieth anniversary of "Grand Ole Opry" in 1985, although, as part of the out-of-court settlement, there was to be another Porter and Dolly recording released, containing only their older material.

True to her word about the Nashville Sound, and *almost* keeping her promise that her next album would be pure country and all her own—two of the songs on the album were the old R&B Esther Phillips hit "Release Me," and the other, released as a single and an immediate hit, was "Single Women," written by Michael O'Donoghue of *The National Lampoon* and "Saturday Night Live" fame—on *Heartbreak Express* Dolly Parton took a backward step—back to the pre-Hollywood Dolly. As she had promised, she recorded it in Nashville, co-producing *Heartbreak Express* with Gregg Perry, her keyboardist, instead of with Gary Klein. This was to be one of her most important albums, especially significant coming directly after the watershed *Nine to Five and Odd Jobs.*

Noel Coppage, *Stereo Review*'s acerbic reviewer, who had trounced the Hollywood albums, was completely won over by the new one, composing a valentine to it headlined "Dolly Parton in Full Flower." "If you grew up, as I did," he wrote, "with the idea that singers are not like you and

me, that singing voices are special, mysterious, a
little foreign, capable of non-ordinary feats, this
album will resonate. Dolly's extraordinary singing style is what it's really about, and there is
simply more of the vocal art going on here than
the ordinary person can keep track of, which
means that one can listen to it again and again
and keep making discoveries. You can come on
home, Dolly. I reckon we're just going to have to
forgive you for them disco records.''

*Heartbreak Express* contained a couple of Dolly's older songs—''My Blue Ridge Mountain Boy,''
''Do I Ever Cross Your Mind,'' and ''Barbara on
Your Mind,'' and some of her newer works, like
''Prime of Your Love,'' ''Heartbreak Express,'' and
''Hollywood Potters,'' but the cleaner, less lush
arrangements and simple vibrato singing was the
old Dolly Parton. It was as though Dolly had
realized what had been missing in her string of
recent ''windup toy'' albums, which even she, in
candid moments, admitted to the press that she
wasn't too crazy about. *Heartbreak Express* was a
concept album about feelings, most of them mel-
ancholy, about Dolly Parton's idea of the sadness
of life and the heartbreak of love in pure music.

There was a running joke between Dolly and
the press, in which she maintained that her husband, Carl, had never heard her music. Or, sometimes, the joke went that Carl had listened to it,
but didn't care for it much, or that he told her she
might amount to something ''someday.'' With
*Heartbreak Express* she admitted for the first time
that her husband was a fan; he really liked this
album. And so did she. It was as though a

pendulum, having swung in a wide arc between country and pop, was finally coming to rest in a true and comfortable center.

One of the major entertainment events of 1981 was Dolly's opening at the Riviera in Las Vegas. The debut was delayed for a couple of days, thanks to Dolly's old devilment, a bad throat and laryngitis. For the show, the Riviera charged $45 for dinner and $35 for cocktails, making the ticket $70, which sounds like an enormous bargain, but not when you consider that, in Vegas, what you save on the meals and entertainment, you lose in the slots and on the wheel.

With Dolly Parton earning $350,000 a week (or $500,000, depending on who was doing the reporting), the inevitable joke quickly flew around town: "That's $175,000 each."

Dolly herself contributed to the wisecracks. "I gotta have a lot of money; you have no idea how expensive industrial bras are." She was quite plump by now, at least 30 pounds overweight, which on a 5-foot frame ("I'm six-four in heels" or "I'd be six-two if it didn't all get so bumped together at the top") was a considerable extra amount for her to carry ("My jeans aren't Jordache, they're lardache.")

Fat or thin or in between, there is only one Dolly Parton, and she wowed the opening night crowd. Her set was a giant fairy-tale castle, complete with drawbridge. Under the musical direction of Gregg Perry, she gave them 78 minutes of her best, including a fantastic takeoff on Elvis Presley in "All Shook Up." It took her two or three numbers before her voice loosened up, thanks to the cortisone injection, but by the time she launched into "Here You Come Again" and "Jolene," followed by "Two Doors Down" and "Coat of Many Colors," Dolly had them eating out of her diamond-ringed hands. When she gave that cynical and savvy audience the sentimental "Me and Little Andy" in that childlike voice, you could hear a tear drop. She sang and sang: "There's No Business Like Show Business," "Nine to Five," which brought down the house, "House of the Rising Sun," and more. When she finally left the stage, cheering fans brought her back for an encore, "I Will Always Love You."

What Dolly Parton accomplished in Las Vegas was what she had meant to accomplish—to bring to the high rollers her unadulterated act, her essential country self, without sellout. While it is true she doesn't use a medieval castle as a backdrop in an ordinary concert, she didn't compromise her material, nor her feelings, nor her religious beliefs.

Dolly Parton was on a roll. It seemed to her and to the world that she couldn't make a wrong step. Every decision she made had worked out well for her. She had made a hit comedy, and it had been a sweetheart filming. Jane Fonda said afterward that Dolly Parton had changed an entire movie crew for the better, and that her spirit and her goodness had made all the others come up a little to meet Dolly's standard, and that the film itself was better because of Dolly.

Dolly had a platinum single and a platinum album in *Nine to Five and Odd Jobs. Heartbreak*

*Express* was on its way to going gold. Her name was up for a couple of Grammys and an Oscar. She was writing furiously, and the songs were good. She was pleasing her critics again. Her Las Vegas opening had been a smash. She was ready to begin shooting her second picture, with the number-one box-office star, the sexy Burt Reynolds. Life was sweet, and was probably going to go on being sweet, and become even sweeter.

What a good thing Dolly Parton didn't have a crystal ball. If she had seen what was in her future, she would have been mighty unhappy!

# *Chapter Eleven*

## The Worst Little Whorehouse in Texas

> There was a lot of blood on this
> project. When it ended, it was the
> most painful thing I had ever done.
>
> —Dolly Parton

Dolly, Lily, and Jane, posing in grinning cama-
raderie, made the January 19, 1981, cover of *People*
magazine. The cover line was: "Dolly Parton: After Her Racy Debut in 9 to 5, Burt Reynolds is
next, but, she insists, 'I'm not selling sex.' "

It took an offer of $1,500,000 and a percentage
of the gross (there is never any net profit, never)
for Dolly Parton to consider doing the R-rated
*The Best Little Whorehouse in Texas*, even though
her male co-star was to be the hottest property in

films and the biggest box-office draw at the moment, Burt Reynolds, whose contract was for $3,500,000 and the inevitable percentage of the gross.

The novel-turned-into-musical-play on which the film was based had been written by Texan Larry L. King, who had co-authored the book of the play and co-authored the original movie script. When the show had opened off-Broadway, the influential syndicated columnist Liz Smith, herself a Texan and devoted to all things bearing the "Texas" brand, was so taken with it that she touted it in her column day after day for months on end, contributing greatly to its success. It was a happy show, revolving around a sixty-two-year-old sheriff and a middle-aged madam, with rollicking songs and cheerful performances. Eventually it would move to Broadway, where it became an even greater hit.

The idea of playing a madam in a picture with "Whorehouse" in its title turned Dolly on, but it also turned her off. When the film was first offered to her, she shook her golden curls no.

"After all, my granddaddy, the Reverend Jake Owens, was a hellfire preacher, and I'm a very religious person," Dolly pointed out. But that was before she went to New York to see the show and had herself a foot-stompin' good time at the bawdy, raunchy hit musical.

"I could just imagine what my family, my religion, and my fans would say," Dolly told *People* magazine. But, after seeing the musical for herself, Dolly changed her mind. "The character's not trash, just caught in this situation. She's probably like I would have been had things been different.

"I said I'd do the picture if the script was rewritten to establish more of a relationship between Miss Mona and Sheriff Earl," Dolly confided to Hollywood reporter and author Bob Thomas. "It would give me a chance to write songs and sing in a picture. I didn't sing a bit in *Nine to Five.* . . . The character of Miss Mona is more like me. I get a chance to dress up the way I like, with the crazy wigs and the wild clothes, and everything juiced up. . . . I like having the freedom of speech in the movie, bein' able to talk the way I talk. I can say *damn* or *hell* if I want to.

"Before I accepted the picture I discussed it with the folks back home, and they all thought it was fine for me to go ahead." Nevertheless, as the film proceeded, Dolly softened Miss Mona's character, against the author's will, just for the folks back home. She gave her role of Miss Mona a Mary Magdalene-type of motivation.

Like all such ventures, Universal-RKO's $20,-000,000-budgeted *The Best Little Whorehouse in Texas* (it eventually would cost $26,000,000; the cost of Dolly's costumes alone shot up over $100,000) began with happy press releases, high hearts, and high hopes. Nobody at that stage could predict that the film would take so long to complete, or make so many people miserable.

The role of Miss Mona Strangely, the madam and owner of the legendary Chicken Ranch of LaGrange, Texas, The Best Little Whorehouse in Texas, seemed to be tailor-made to suit Dolly's looks and talent. The author, Larry King, thought that casting Dolly Parton was just *too* obvious. "She looks like she might run a whorehouse or work in one," he growled.

Dolly admitted publicly that she had always had a "thing" for Burt Reynolds ("I don't want to miss a chance with Burt").

Conversely, Burt leered publicly that he always had a "thing" for her, and would be glad to show her what it was. "She's sweet and pure as the driven snow mounds, and I can't wait to begin work. Dolly Parton was made to be a movie star."

Seriously, Burt had been after Dolly professionally ever since he had filmed *W. W. and the Dixie Dancekings*. He had wanted her for that film, and wanted to do a picture with her for years. A press release went out stating that Burt Reynolds had refused to do *Whorehouse* unless Dolly Parton was signed for the role of Miss Mona, at the same time that Dolly was refusing the film unless Burt Reynolds played Sheriff Earl Ed! What a happy coincidence! How believable!

As usual with a big-budget picture that depended on "bankable" names, changes had been made in the script to accommodate the stars, and they made the writer, Larry L. King, furious. Sheriff Earl Ed Dodd—played by Reynolds, of course—would no longer be sixty-two years old, but thirty-five (Burt was then forty-six). There would be love scenes between Dolly and Burt, although there had been no love scenes in the musical play. Dolly wanted to be in charge of the music, although the film was to include the original score of the musical show, written by Carol Hall.

In fact, King was so angry with the way the

project was going that he offered to punch Reynolds out, an offer that seems never to have been taken up. Also, good newspaperman that he was, Larry King kept a journal of the making of the film, and Viking Press published it as *The Whorehouse Papers*. In the book, King accused Reynolds of wanting to make *Smokey and the Bandit Go to a Whorehouse*, and charged Dolly with throwing her considerable weight around to get several of her songs added to the Carol Hill score, and for pushing for love scenes between herself and Reynolds.

"Wouldn't you feel like you was cheated if you paid five dollars for a ticket and then didn't get to see me and Burt Reynolds kissin'?" she demanded. But Dolly went on record immediately to state that nudity and graphic sex were two mammoth Parton no-no's.

"When I say love scenes, I'm talkin' about holding, hugging, kissing, and things that make sense. I could never do a nude scene. I'm not selling sex," she told *People*, which stuck the line on the cover of the magazine. "The magic of the whole thing is that I am one way and look another."

Dolly Parton had never made a secret of her fascination for whores. She has even said that the trademark way she dresses owes a lot to the prostitutes she saw as a girl.

"I always liked the look of our hookers back home. Their big hairdos and makeup made them look more. When people say less is more, I say more is more. Less is less. I go for more."

To Chet Flippo of *Rolling Stone*, Dolly added, "Some of my best friends have been hussies or called whores because they are usually the most honest and open people. And, even if they don't do it as a profession, I just relate to it, and I've often said that I honestly do look like a whore or a high-class prostitute, not even so much high class, with the makeup and the bleached hair and the boobs and the tight-fittin' clothes and the high heels ... except that I'm not a whore. But if I hadn't made it in this business, who knows?" She also said mischievously, "I make a better whore than a secretary."

"Prostitutes," Dolly told Cliff Jahr in the *Ladies' Home Journal* after the picture was completed, "are some of the sweetest, most caring people I've known because they've been through everything! I've met them at parties, and I've talked with them. Usually, they're people with broken dreams who never had a chance in life or were sexually abused or ignored as children. A lot sell themselves to get some kind of feeling of being loved. The movie will show these women have feelings. You're gonna cry your eyes out."

*The Best Little Whorehouse in Texas* was shot at Universal Studios in Los Angeles and on location, in Halletsville and Pflugerville, Texas, and soon the word was out in the press that things were not going along so merrily with the production. It was a problem picture. There was a series of changes in producers and directors. Two directors—Tommy Tune and Peter Masterson, who had directed the original New York show—were fired. The final director of the film was Colin Higgins, who had directed and co-written the script

of *Nine to Five*. One set was pulled down and
built over again from the ground up.

"Each time they changed," said Dolly, "I had to
write new songs, forty or fifty in all." Although she
fought like a tiger to defend her songs, only two
of them actually made it into the finished film—
a duet with Burt Reynolds, "Sneakin' Around,"
and an old song of hers, "I Will Always Love
You," which was released as a single and which
she had already adopted as her signature encore
number. However, she did record the soundtrack
album.

What was the core of the problem? Most of the
insiders agreed that it wasn't a "what" but a
"who," Burt Reynolds. Reynolds had become
moody and difficult, "a nightmare" to work with,
making demands, pushing people around, storm-
ing off the set. He had recently broken off with
his lover, Sally Field, and it had been a long and
very close relationship. Earnings on his last three
pictures had been disappointing; Reynolds hadn't
been achieving in the recent years the success he
was accustomed to, and he was running scared.

In particular, Reynolds appeared to be afraid
that the buxom, earthy Dolly, with a role she
could sink her teeth into, might prove to be fun-
nier than he, and walk off with the picture. There
is nothing in the world more perilous to an established star than to have a picture stolen from him
by a comparative amateur. The bigger egos are,
the more fragile.

"On the movie, we've gone through so much
bitterness—tensions, quarrels, hurt feelings. I
threatened to quit so many times," said Dolly. "I

don't ever want to work that hard again. There's this tiny voice in me that keeps saying, 'This is the last movie you'll ever make.' "

When Bob Thomas asked her why, Dolly replied, "Well, it's hard to make compromises, and that's what you gotta do in this business. I don't want to lose my values. The only way I would do another picture was if I could maintain control of the project. That way I could be sure of workin' with the people I wanted to work with. On a picture you're dealin' with so many people and bendin' so much that you lose control."

Caught between Larry L. King's bitter attacks and Burt Reynolds's sulks and temper tantrums, never knowing from day to day when she would have to work with a brand-new producer or director, Dolly Parton must have longed for the good old days when she, Lily, and Jane were giggling over herbal tea and swapping the names of designers and directors. *Nine to Five* had been "a blessed thing" and "the best experience I could have had." *The Best Little Whorehouse in Texas* caused Dolly "more problems, sorrows, and enlightenment" than she had ever known before. Making the film "was a real painful thing," she said. As an experience, it was "the worst."

"It's been kind of a bloodbath all the way through. The people who wrote it got ushered out, and so many people changed—they just weren't right for the picture, so they had to be fired. Well, it just hurt me real bad. I saw so much compromising being done, it just about killed me emotionally."

But Dolly Parton always takes the fabric of her

life—it doesn't matter if it's rosy or black—and stitches it into something artistic and beautiful. This time was no different. Something of the agony she experienced making *The Best Little Whorehouse in Texas* came out in a song on her twenty-eighth album, *Heartbreak Express*. In "Hollywood Potters" Dolly described Hollywood poetically as the "dungeon of drama, the center of sorrow, the city of schemes, the terrace of trauma, the palace of promises and the dealer of dreams."

Most interviews she gave regarding *The Best Little Whorehouse in Texas* quoted her as being understanding about Burt Reynolds's problems, no matter how they may have impacted on her personally. But there was no question but that she gave almost as good as she got; inside that blond fluff and under those curves is a core of stainless steel.

"People think of me as all smiles," she told *People*, but I can get aggravated. When I got somethin' to say, I'll say it." Some of the things that she and Reynolds said to each other "brought tears to his or my eyes." But "we agreed that we would stick together no matter what. If he left the picture, I'd leave. If I left, he'd leave. We knew it was going to be a very big movie, and that we had to stick it out."

And yet, despite the tempers and the temperaments, despite the harsh tear-inducing words, a large number of people in the press and on the set of the picture are convinced that Dolly Parton and Burt Reynolds were lovers during and for a short while after the making of *The Best Little Whorehouse in Texas*. They point to passionate kisses that continued after the cameras stopped rolling, to a trip the two of them took together; the supermarket tabloids ran screaming headlines that had the pair sneaking off to a private tête-à-tête in Burt's Florida hideaway. They also wrote that Burt had spent several nights in Las Vegas when Dolly Parton debuted there.

"Dolly Parton Agrees to Have Burt Reynolds's Baby!" screamed the headlines, ironically, for, as it would soon be known, Dolly wasn't in the physical shape to have anybody's baby.

Were those nights in Las Vegas a love tryst for Dolly Parton and Burt Reynolds? Dolly, needless to say, issued the usual denial. Admitting that she had been tempted ("I'm not dead yet"), she added, "We didn't have enough of that to spoil our friendship. Besides, I'm a married woman." Once more, Carl Dean was conveniently there.

But Dolly and Carl were spending more time together than usual. During the filming of Nine to Five, Carl had come to Los Angeles, a city he normally avoided, and stayed with Dolly in her new, rented two-bedroom Beverly Hills digs. When The Best Little Whorehouse in Texas finally wrapped, Dolly and Carl went off to Australia together for a short holiday. Was it to quell the rumors about Dolly and Burt? Or maybe was it to make up for the business visit to Australia that Dolly had taken in February, to look at potential real estate?

With her manager, Sandy Gallin, Dolly had gone land-shopping by helicopter, scouting beachfront property for another of her many houses. The trip occasioned many rumors of an affair between them.

It seems that every time Dolly Parton works closely with a man, "affair" is the word on everybody's lips but hers. Dolly swears her relationship with Gallin is strictly platonic; they are partners in several ventures.

"I do have a right to some secret spots," Dolly told Cliff Jahr about a month before *Whorehouse* opened in the summer of 1982. Dolly had had some personal problems in 1981—an "affair of the heart, not a love affair," she hinted mysteriously, refusing to name the person. There was speculation that the person was Porter Wagoner, and that the problem was the $3,000,000 legal suit he launched against her that year to recover royalties. These business problems were an emotional body blow to Dolly; she felt betrayed, and the prospect of a public lawsuit made her feel quite ill.

"It just about killed me. I cried an ocean. Then also last year my throat was bad. I was trying to write, there were lots of family problems, and this came on top of all the movie's putdowns and dragouts and misunderstandings. Suddenly, six months into the year, everything switched, cleared up, and turned into a year of enlightenment. It will happen again, I'm sure, in seven years when I'm forty-two." Actually, in seven years Dolly would be forty-three, but perhaps her memory had slipped a year.

Dolly's throat wasn't her only physical problem; far, far worse lay ahead of her. Dolly and Sandy Gallin had to cut their Australia trip short, because she was suffering severe pain. As soon as she and Gallin came back from Australia, Dolly went into a hospital in Los Angeles for what was termed "minor" gynecological surgery.

For years, Dolly Parton had been struggling with health problems connected with her menstrual cycle. Under the gun on the set of *The Best Little Whorehouse in Texas*, she had been suffering for about 6 months with terrible headaches and excruciating cramps. What she called "my woman's problem" and "my hormone imbalance" had already forced her to cancel her 1982 Las Vegas appearance, an Atlantic City engagement, and a string of other concerts, including Houston, Cleveland, and Merrillville, Indiana. Because the picture was taking so much longer to wrap than was scheduled, Dolly had put off doing anything about her worsening physical condition, and had let the problem go a little too far.

Dolly's illness, plus the anguish involved in *Whorehouse*, had caused the usually optimistic, positive-thinking Dolly Parton to suffer a most uncharacteristic depression, which accounts somewhat for the *tristesse* of the songs on *Heartbreak Express*.

It was everyone's hope that minor surgery would relieve the condition, and avoid a complete hysterectomy. Although Dolly Parton was thirty-six and had been married sixteen years without children, and although the likelihood of Dolly and Carl's having children was remote in any case, a hysterectomy is a drastic step for any woman. "I didn't want to have the complete job done. I was hopin' that a lot of it was just overwork and mental anguish. I was under a lot of stress, and out of balance."

Dolly entered St. John's Hospital in Santa Monica on Monday, February 15, 1982. Since the operation was minor (the nature of it was not disclosed, but it was most likely a dilation curettage) she was out of the hospital only a day or two later.

Her physician's post-surgery recommendation was "complete rest away from work and other strenuous chores for at least four to six weeks."

After the operation, Dolly and Carl went to Tara, where Dolly recuperated for a few months. The original plan was for Dolly to go back to work by the end of April, but she didn't recover as quickly as was expected, so she canceled her bookings for May and June, too. There was some concern that she might not be well enough for the gala premiere in July of *The Best Little Whorehouse in Texas*.

When Dolly's song "Nine to Five" won two Grammy awards—the songwriting award for Best Country Song, and the Best Female Country Performance—and was a finalist in two other categories—Best Song of the Year, and Best Album of Original Score Written for a Motion Picture or TV Special, a nomination she shared with Charles Fox—Dolly couldn't attend the ceremonies in Los Angeles.

Because she was still filming *Whorehouse*, Dolly had missed out on the ceremonies the previous October, when Broadcast Music Incorporated had given "Nine to Five" the Robert J. Burton Award for the Most Performed Song of the Year in both the country and pop categories. Dolly had to be content with sending BMI a wire saying, "I'm thrilled. Songwriting is my heart and soul."

But Dolly's attitude was, operation or no operation, recuperation be damned; she wasn't going to sit around on her duff forever. When the American Guild of Variety Artists (AGVA) presented her with two honors, the Female Country Star of the Year and the Entertainer of the Year awards at their May telecast, Dolly Parton was there wearing rhinestoned bells. AGVA had honored her twice before, in 1978 and 1979 as Country Star of the Year, but this time they gave her their highest accolade, Entertainer of the Year, and she wasn't about to miss that as she had missed the Grammys.

At the end of June 1982, Dolly announced a new deal in Nashville. She had assigned Tree International, the music publishing company that had taken her in years ago, when she was but a young hopeful, to manage her song publishing. To Tree she assigned over 900 songs, past and present, for management and administration. The deal included Dolly's own material and those of other songwriters in her stable at her companies Velvet Apple and Song Yard, including her siblings Randy, Rachel, and Frieda, songs by her Uncle Bill Owens, and around 100 Frank Dycus songs. Copyrights were not involved in the deal, and the song catalog to be managed by Tree did not include the songs still in the Combine Music catalog, songs written between 1966 and 1968.

The purpose of this deal was ostensibly to reduce Dolly's overhead by consolidating her publishing with a fully staffed company, but in fact it was another way of freeing Dolly Parton from some of her earlier family ties. Relationships with some of the kinfolk working for her had become too tangled and strained, and the new Dolly, with her new management, was oppressed by the old constraints. Also, it added to the tension she had experienced with Burt Reynolds and *The Best Little Whorehouse in Texas*.

The film opened at a televised gala premiere in Austin, Texas, in August 1982. Dolly was there, looking terrific, and apparently feeling great, although in actuality she wasn't at all well.

In its review, *Variety* said the picture "ideally teams powerhouse stars Burt Reynolds and Dolly Parton, a combo which should please mass audiences thoroughly. Film delivers on all the traditional levels of popular entertainment, so there's no reason it shouldn't prove a substantial box-office winner...." As usual, *Variety* was prophetic. *The Best Little Whorehouse in Texas* went on to become the third top-grossing movie musical, grossing $87,000,000 at the box office alone, not counting foreign sales and video, and proved to be a success for everybody. Liz Smith hated it, and said so in her column. But then, Liz is a friend of Larry L. King's.

As for Dolly, she was quoted as saying, "This was a picture that got way, way out of hand. There was a lot of blood spilled just turnin' it from a Broadway show into a picture. The fightin' was real terrible. I feel real bad about how Burt and Larry King kept fightin' it out in the press. But I don't regret anythin' I ever do. If nothin' else, it's a good experience, and it teaches me a lot."

What it taught her was that, in Hollywood, if you don't have control of a project, then you're nothing but a hired hand, no matter how high your salary.

The release of *The Best Little Whorehouse in Texas* as well as the release of the soundtrack album and *Heartbreak Express*, the album on which she'd "cried an ocean," was the customary occasion for a tour. Dolly scheduled an 8-week, 35-stop tour of the U.S. and Canada. As usual, she had taken on enough play-dates to wreck the health of a younger, stronger person, but that was always Dolly's way. She was fat, unhealthy, and unhappy, and she thought that what she needed most in the world was to get out there and work. Besides, she had canceled a lot of play-dates earlier in the year, and it was time to make good on them.

"Nothing beats getting out on the stage and singing direct to my fans, the people who've been my friends all through the years, plus the new friends I've met along the way." What Dolly loves best are the plain folk who wash up the supper dishes and come to see her shows.

For her fourth concert in the series, Dolly Parton was scheduled to sing at the Ohio State Fair in Columbus. Her fee: $50,000. Suddenly, she began hemorrhaging internally. Doctors advised her strongly against going on, but Dolly wouldn't listen. She not only played and sang both a matinee and evening concert, but insisted on going forward to her next concert, the fifth of the 35, on Sunday, August 22, 1982, at the Indiana State Fair in Indianapolis. She spent a really bad night on her bus between Columbus and Indianapolis. The internal bleeding, with intestinal complications, started up again, but she didn't change her mind. These people had paid to hear her sing, and sing she would. She even counted on playing the dates after Indianapolis—the Houston, Texas, Rodeo, Merrillville, Indiana, and Cleveland, Ohio— bookings she had canceled when she entered the hospital for her earlier surgery, in February.

There was a ferocious, driving rainstorm at the Indianapolis fairgrounds, but her fans didn't seem to mind. No one left. They sat enraptured in the rain, not even noticing that they were getting soaked through to the bone. Once more, doctors warned her that to go on was foolhardy and dangerous, but she paid them no heed. Dressed in a glittery sequined gown with long fringes on the sleeves, Dolly gave them what they wanted— "Jolene," "Coat of Many Colors," her standard encore of "I Will Always Love You"—the songs with which she was most identified. Although Dolly herself was under a canopy, the pelting rain swept in to drench her, chilling her through. She was also hemorrhaging internally with abdominal bleeding, but the audience of 8,000 fans never suspected.

Because Dolly was afraid she might be forced to cut the concert short because of the weather and her physical condition, she had rescheduled her biggest numbers to go right at the beginning, so that her listeners wouldn't go away disappointed. She played the concert through to its cheering ovation, then came offstage and collapsed, doubling over in agony.

Hours later, Dolly was on a plane to New York, to undergo confidential tests at an unnamed hospital. The balance of her tour through mid-September was canceled on orders from her physicians. Carl Dean flew in from Nashville to be at her side.

A publicity spokesperson issued a statement: "She has tried to forestall surgery at all costs in the past, but now just about every doctor she talks to advises her to have it."

"I never again want to postpone my personal or professional life because of these problems," announced Dolly from her New York apartment while waiting for her doctor's verdict about whether she would have to undergo surgery, although it was evident that this time minor surgery would do little to relieve her condition. It would have to be major. "Thank the Lord that Carl and I never wanted children that bad." But, Dolly being Dolly, she also tried looking at the bright side. "It was God's way of sayin', 'Sit down and think about everything.' Before that, I had always gone full blast." Now she was praying, calling on the Lord for help and strength.

When the inevitable verdict was given—that Dolly Parton should go under the knife for a major operation—she flew to Los Angeles and had it done. Exactly what surgical procedure followed was never announced, but speculation had it that the operation had stopped just short of a complete hysterectomy.

The operation left her weak; it would take Dolly months of complete rest to recover. Between the medication and the inactivity, she gained more weight, 30 pounds more. She had endured a year of pain, bad health, tension, anger, and frustration. Not to mention that mysterious broken heart that had made Dolly "cry an ocean."

Just talking about it to *People* magazine depressed Dolly. "That was a real hard one for me—when you've always been the rock and then you turn to sand."

She told syndicated writer Jack Hurst, "I just wasn't in such a radiant mood as I have been in the past. A lot of people think I'm all sunshine and flowers. But I've had my share of sorrow. I just seem to handle it better than other people do. I refuse to waller in it."

Although Dolly Parton's health worries were behind her, other troubles were really only beginning.

# *Chapter Twelve*

## Dolly, How Could You?

I thought Stallone and I would be good together, the way I thought Burt Reynolds and I would be good together. But I didn't finish singing a song in the whole movie, and I don't think people want to see Stallone with his shirt on.

—Dolly Parton

To Dolly Parton, the road was life, heartsblood. She always thrived on performing before thousands, hearing them call out requests for their favorite songs, seeing people leaving her concerts with their spirits refreshed. Touring in her big, comfortable $180,000 tour bus with the boys made a restless Dolly happy.

In late January 1983, Dolly Parton quit the road.

The trouble began a week or so earlier, with death threats that forced her to cancel her concerts, 10 play-dates into a 31-city tour. Dolly and the band had been booked into the Executive Inn in Rivermont, just outside Owensboro, Kentucky, for 2 sold-out, $52-per-ticket appearances.

Ninety minutes before she was to go onstage, an anonymous female caller phoned the Owensboro police and told them that Dolly was in danger of being killed "by a man who hates the ground Dolly walks on." The woman went on to say the potential assassin believed that Dolly "had done him wrong." Refusing to give police the man's name, the caller stated, "I can't tell you who he is. He'll kill me and my family."

Many celebrities are targets of death threats by mentally disturbed people who believe they have a grievance, or even by stupid pranksters with nothing better to do with their time. But this was Dolly's third death threat in recent months, and the police were taking it very seriously. They were afraid she was being stalked by somebody, perhaps by an ex-con who, misunderstanding Dolly's lyrics, took her songs to be about him personally. He also seemed to be laboring under the delusion that Dolly had once been married to him.

Under the advice of the police, Dolly canceled the Executive Inn concerts, but not until 15 minutes before show time. This gave her time to get herself and her band back into the tour bus and leave the grounds secretly. Dolly left Kentucky under police escort, going from the city police to the state police, then to the Kentucky–Tennessee border, where Tennessee authorities took over. Dolly headed straight to Nashville and Carl.

"We don't take chances with Dolly," said a Parton spokesperson, who added that her Nashville manager Don Wharton had hired detectives to track down the threatener. The case was never solved.

"Dolly was real upset," said band member Don Rutledge. "She couldn't go onstage thinking someone would actually try that and maybe shoot one of us or something. It just really freaked her out."

Dolly went into seclusion, beefed up the security at her home, hired a bodyguard, and canceled the rest of her January dates—concerts in New Orleans, Fort Worth, and Beaumont, Texas. At the same time, an announcement was made to the press that Dolly Parton would lay off her band and quit the road after her London concert in March. The London concert was a biggie, because it was taped live for a 90-minute Home Box Office cable special, "Dolly Parton in Concert," which was seen in June 1983, tied in with RCA Records' cross-promotion of Dolly's new album, *Burlap and Satin*, released in late May, containing some of the numbers from Dolly's cable-TV debut.

Among the songs on the album were "Send Me the Pillow You Dream On," "Appalachian Memories," "Gamble Either Way," "I Really Don't Want to Know," and a very upbeat number, "Oo-Eee."

"She has plans for movies for five or six months," said Dolly's publicist, Katie Valk. "So there will be a long block of time with no touring. There's a possibility that she'll do two films back to back during that time." Dolly actually stayed off the road for 18 months, a record for her.

Dolly laid low for a few months, taking the time to think, write songs, read a lot of books, and go to Hawaii, a favorite place of hers, where she bought yet another home, a vacation retreat on Oahu. At the same time she bought herself a nightclub, the Blue Indigo on Oahu. She was disheartened, tired, almost suicidal, as she would later reveal to the press. She determined to choose her next projects with the greatest care. Among them for 1984 were an album, a TV Christmas special, and a tour with beloved country-crossover star Kenny Rogers. Meanwhile she prayed, asking the Lord what she should do next. The connection must have been bad, or maybe the lines got crossed, because Dolly thought that God said "Go thou and make a movie called *Rhinestone*."

Once again, as she did with *Nine to Five*, she dubbed her upcoming film "a blessed project," with much less reason, as it turned out. As a business decision, making *Rhinestone* was somewhere on a par with changing the formula for Coca-Cola.

Sylvester Stallone had never made a comedy or a musical, and there was no reason on earth to believe he could do either. But that didn't stop him. In fact, it kind of nurtured the plot, if one can use the term "plot" for so creaky and predictable a set of circumstances. The plot of *Rhinestone*

was based on one of the oldest gags in the
world—"I bet I can take the next person who
walks by the door and, in only two weeks, I'll
turn him into a star!" In this case, the "next
person" was Sly Stallone, a New York cabbie,
and the person making the boast (and the bet)
was Dolly Parton, who was then forced to turn
this lumpish piece of "dese-dem-and-dose" pro-
toplasm, who cannot sing a note, into a country
music star.

Dolly Parton had vowed never to make a picture again unless she had control, but *Rhinestone*
was Sylvester Stallone's personal project for Twentieth Century-Fox. It had been originally conceived
as a modest film to be based on the great song by
Larry Weiss, "Rhinestone Cowboy." That was before Rocky got his mitts on it. Stallone had co-
authored the screenplay with Phil Aldon Robinson,
and Fox, hoping it was backing another of the
Stallone blockbusters, had given Sly a huge budget. Paramount, which had dropped a bundle on
the Stallone-directed turkey *Staying Alive* a couple of years later, must have snickered at Fox's
naïveté. A nonviolent Sylvester Stallone sells no
tickets.

So Dolly settled for musical control, and for
getting Sandy Gallin and their partner, Ray Katz,
in as executive producers. She was determined to
keep musical control, because Stallone's brother,
Frank, is a singer and a songwriter, and Dolly
didn't want him muscling in.

The first thing Dolly did was perhaps a bit
ill-advised. She canceled her summer tour. This
was the concert tour that was to have made up

for the concert tour she had canceled when she received those death threats and quit the road. The tour, which would have included the cities she had canceled out the previous year, was supposed to have started in July and run through the middle of August, 25 play-dates in 20 cities. The reason Dolly gave was that she had to prepare for *Rhinestone*. Because a film rider was part of her touring contract, the promoters had to let her cancel without penalty. Earlier cancellations had led to lawsuits on the part of the outraged bookers and promoters who had been forced to give back enormous sums for unused tickets. Was Dolly Parton burning her bridges? Would she ever concertize again? Or was she becoming reclusive, going "Hollywood"?

There was some talk that Dolly might be hurting herself in the concert markets by her repeated cancellations. But Dolly was far more interested in getting ready to compose and record the *Rhinestone* soundtrack. She also canceled some scheduled television appearances, wishing to reserve all her energies for the picture; on this film she would be musical director, writing and supervising the film's original music score and soundtrack album. According to the press, she was also consulting with Stallone on any additional material for the script. Dolly Parton was learning very rapidly how to escalate her control and her production participation.

"I am very excited and looking forward to a wonderful creative partnership with Sly," purred Dolly. "From the beginning of my career, my goal has been full involvement with, and artistic control of, the movies I make."

Sly Stallone purred back. "There is no one I feel more secure with and inspired by than the incredible Dolly Parton."

When, after her illness and a long hiatus, Dolly Parton finally began working again, she started writing and soon got up a full head of steam. Returning to Nashville in August 1983, to get back in touch with her country music roots, within 3 weeks she had written the 13 songs that were used in *Rhinestone*, plus 7 additional ones.

"Those songs just fell into my lap," she said happily. "I was feelin' just great again, just to get that old energy goin'."

Dolly told *People*, "I thought, since these are country songs, I should go to Nashville and in and around Kentucky. I went home and took my camper and my girl friend Judy Ogle, who's always with me." Dolly's best friend Judy acts as Dolly's personal assistant and has devoted her life to being with Dolly Parton.

"We'd just go out and sit on the riverbank and just park and check into these dinky little motels, which I love to do anyway. When I finished, I told those producers, 'Look, these are the songs and this is exactly what we need. Now, if anybody wants anything different, don't come to me.' "

Mindful of her family, Dolly brought in some of her kin to work on the the production. Two of her brothers—Randy and Floyd, who used to be with the Travelin' Family Band—were heard on the soundtrack and were also seen singing "Waltz

Me to Heaven" on the screen. Friends also joined in, including Speck Rhodes, the toothless comic of "The Porter Wagoner Show."

Sylvester Stallone, more body-conscious than any Miss America, lost 40 pounds before going before the cameras. Dolly, whose weight was up there in the stratosphere, was aghast. "He's so self-disciplined, I tell you, if anybody told me to lose forty pounds for a movie, I'd say, 'You can kiss my country ass.'"

Still, Sly's regimen and his diet set Dolly to thinking. She was more than 30 pounds overweight, thanks to the medications she had taken and the inactivity caused by her long illness. She had had to watch her weight since the age of twenty-eight or twenty-nine. Her diet consisted largely of fried foods and starches; she was also a junk-food junkie, and she loved to eat. Now at thirty-eight, she poked fun at her embonpoint, saying, "My fat ain't never lost me no money." Yet, inside was a thin person crying to be released.

As the picture got under way, it seemed to be jinxed from the start. The first director was Don Zimmerman, a friend of Stallone's who, up until Rhinestone, had only been a film editor. Less than a month into the picture, Zimmerman left. With him went three and a half weeks of shooting. The new director, brought in to replace Zimmerman, was Bob Clark, whose claim to fame was Porky's, a gross film, perhaps, but an even grosser grosser.

"I'd heard a lot of stories about Sylvester Stallone, that he was impossible," admitted Dolly.

"The chances of it working out were pretty remote," admitted Stallone.

But the two of them "got their shit together up front," in Dolly's words, and the filming proceeded more calmly than expected. Dolly told Sylvester Stallone right up front that she wasn't going to stand for his dumping on her with the same unbridled criticism he heaped on others, or taking out his black moods on her. "But I could hardly wait to see who he was goin' to fire or cuss out next. He was smart, though, and it was never me."

The problems were not with the stars' egos, and the problems were not with the direction. The problem lay in the fact that the film was ever made at all. A bummer with a terrible script, *Rhinestone* wound up costing Fox big bucks it didn't earn back.

Market research showed that Sylvester Stallone fans did not want to see him with Dolly Parton, and that Dolly Parton fans did not want to see her with Sylvester Stallone. A three-year-old could have predicted it. There was no chemistry between them—zilch. Stallone was too wooden and Dolly too animated; it was as though each of them was playing in a different film at the same time. Only an actor with a flair for comedy could have brought off a script as bad as *Rhinestone*'s, and Sylvester Stallone did not possess that flair. Besides which, he couldn't sing a note, even with the voluptuous coaching of Dolly Parton for two fun-filled weeks.

Dolly's third film, which opened in July 1984,

was a total disaster, a big-budget stinkeroo, a box-office bomb. Heads rolled.

*Variety*, that bible of show biz, lamented "Mismatched Sly and Dolly in an off-the-wall comedy." *Variety* went on to say, "Effortlessly living up to its title, *Rhinestone* is as artificial and synthetic a concoction as has ever made its way to the screen. . . . Neither Stallone nor Parton strays at all from their past personae, and major shows are actually put on by their costume designers, since the two leads seem to change their clothes every three minutes [which, considering how tight they fit, is no small achievement]. . . ."

Of all the deservedly abysmal reviews that *Rhinestone* received, Kip Kirby's in her "Nashville Scene" column in *Billboard* was among the most eloquent. Ms. Kirby's review was headlined, "Dolly, How Could You?" It read, in part, "It's baffling to try to figure an explanation for Dolly Parton's association with *Rhinestone*, a film which could set the image of country music—not to mention the South—back ten years. *Rhinestone* parodies everything connected with country, portraying its entertainers as hicks and its fans as stereotyped obnoxious boors. . . . Why would Dolly, who has personally done so much to upgrade country's image around the world, appear in a film which reinforces every miserable negative that country music has had to fight against . . . ? Dolly's presence in *Rhinestone* lends credibility to a project that is an embarrassment to many people in the country entertainment industry."

Stallone was devastated, but Dolly was a lot more philosophical. "Sly probably thinks I wrecked his career with that movie, but to me, I was the one taking the chance. I've done *two* musicals with men who can't sing—Sly and Burt Reynolds—and here I am a singer. Both were bad casting, of course, but I have only myself to blame.

"He's pretty to look at, too," said Dolly to Cliff Jahr, "and I know that when Sasha, his last wife, was getting her divorce, she said we were having an affair. Not true at all. Sly and I are just not each other's type. Both he and Burt are egomaniacs, but Sly is the perfect balance of total ego and total insecurity. I see how his mind works. If you were in love with him, he'd pick out all your weaknesses and either use them to help you or use them against you."

Dolly hasn't made a film since *Rhinestone*, but "I think I will do movies again," she says. "The people seem to like me in them, and I guess I owe it to them. But I don't have the kind of stars in my eyes anymore that could lead me to destruction. I see movie pictures as a business, and it ought to be run that way. If and when I do a picture in the future, I'm definitely gonna be involved in the producing end of things. I'll probably write the story, too. I'm gonna have a lot more control than I've had up to now, and I'm gonna use it."

For a couple of years now, Dolly Parton has been promising a film project that would reunite her with her old buddies Lily Tomlin and Jane Fonda. Not a sequel to *Nine to Five*, but an adventure comedy. But so far, a script has not come together.

Dolly Parton is never one to look behind her, only ahead. So, after the catastrophe of *Rhinestone*, she picked herself up, dusted herself off, and went on with her life. Much was happening.

For one thing, she began losing the extra weight she had picked up over the years. She started out by doing "everything"—she fasted, went on liquid protein, did the Dr. Atkins diet, all the quick-weight-loss programs that one cannot stay on forever because they are too dangerous. Then, as the pounds began to melt away, Dolly discovered the secret of her own dieting success. She began to eat again the foods she loved, anything she wanted or craved, only in tiny portions. A bite or two, not the whole thing. She ate numerous little tiny meals, and still she lost weight. "I'm in hog heaven," she crowed. She lost 10 pounds, 20, 30, until she was back to the old zaftig Dolly. But then Dolly went on, until today, to the point where she has lost a total of 50 pounds. She is 5 feet tall, and weighs 100 pounds, most of it, as she'll be the first to tell you, above the waist.

In March 1983, Monument Records and Combine Music, Dolly Parton's first record company of so many years ago, filed for bankruptcy under Chapter XI, citing $7,300,000 in debts and $8,-800,000 in assets. In November 1984, an investment group consisting of LeFrak Entertainment Ltd. of New York, Lorimar Productions, and Dolly Parton filed a reorganization plan for Monument and offered to buy Fred Foster's 70 percent interest in the company for $4,900,000 and Bob Beckham's 30 percent interest for $2,100,000, a total of $7,000,000. An additional $1,000,000 was offered for the company's master recordings and the Monument-Combine building, owned by Fred Foster, on Music Row in Nashville. The eighteen-year-old girl with the cardboard suitcase filled with songs was now a multimillionaire superstar, ready to buy back and reorganize the company herself. She was identified to the Bankruptcy Court as having a net worth "of not less than five million dollars," although of course it is a lot more than that.

It was Dolly's intention to be actively involved in the management of both Monument and Combine, to reactivate the company, pay off the creditors—among whom were Roy Orbison, Kris Kristofferson's producer David Anderle, Larry Gatlin, Rita Coolidge, Jennie Seely, and Dolly Parton—and make the company into a country music giant. It had an enviable catalog—included in the Monument archives were hits by Roy Orbison, Larry Gatlin, Tony Joe White, and others, including Dolly Parton's "Dumb Blonde," and a duet that Dolly had recorded in 1982 with Willie Nelson, "Everything Is Beautiful In Its Own Way," from Nelson's *The Winning Hand* album. Combine, the music-publishing arm of the firm, was a treasure trove of classics and was the successful end of the business.

It's a shame the deal didn't go through; if it had, it would have made Dolly Parton one of the three or four biggest music-publishing outfits in

Music City, U.S.A. And Monument Records, for whom she planned to record her new material, would be on top of the heap.

In the fall of 1984, two giants of country music got together again—Dolly Parton and Kenny Rogers. In 1983, they had recorded "Islands in the Stream," for Rogers's first album on the RCA label, *Eyes That See in the Dark*, a collaboration that made the Rogers album go platinum, while the song itself went to the number-one slot on all the charts, country as well as pop, and became the most-played, most-requested song of the year, as well as the best-selling single, going platinum. It was one of the biggest hits of both their long careers.

"You pray for a song like 'Islands in the Stream' to come along," said Rogers. "The most wonderful thing about it was the chance to sing with Dolly. As soon as we'd finished recording it, I knew it was going to be an enormous hit." The song won the Song of the Year Award at the 1984 presentations of the Country Music Association, and was named BMI-Nashville's Most Performed Song of the Year. It also sold more than 2,000,000 copies of the single, and pushed the Rogers album over the platinum 1,000,000 mark.

Having tasted success together, the two superstars went on for the full meal. Actually, they had talked for years about working together on projects and even a road tour, but Dolly's ill health and the three pictures she had made had not allowed her to commit any of her time to Kenny Rogers.

215

But now, a Christmas album, *Kenny Rogers' and Dolly Parton's Once Upon a Christmas*, also went platinum faster than you could say "Kenny 'n' Dolly."

That was all they needed to inspire them. At the tail end of 1984, Kenny and Dolly launched into megabucks, what *Variety* called "a major creative combination," a one-hour TV Christmas special, "Kenny & Dolly: A Christmas to Remember," originated for them by CBS and obviously based on the success of the earlier album. The TV special, which aired December 2, 1984, featured 5 original Dolly Parton songs, as well as such standards as "White Christmas" and "Silent Night," and a group of animated elves who stole the show. It was a co-production of Dolly's company, Speckled Bird Productions, and Kenny's company, Lion Share Productions. Both the stars' personal managers—Sandy Gallin for Dolly, and Ken Kragen for Kenny—were named as producers. It goes without saying that the RCA album of the show, more than 1,000,000 copies of *Kenny Rogers' and Dolly Parton's Once Upon a Christmas*, were in the record stores during Thanksgiving week, and went platinum, predictably, without delay.

What's more, the superstar pair was going on the road together, as one of the most eagerly awaited package acts ever. It had been more than a year since Dolly's health problems had forced her to cancel and give up her last bus tour, and some two and a half years since she had managed to finish any of her tours. This equal-billing tour started off December 28 at the Oakland, California, Coliseum, and was to carry Dolly and Kenny through 42 cities until the end of March, including a big-ticket New Year's Eve gala at the Los Angeles Forum, with seats selling for $30 and $50.

One of the New York City concerts in March was played for the benefit of the African Relief Fund, as part of Kenny Rogers's ongoing commitment to the cause of world hunger.

Dolly Parton was on the road again.

# *Chapter Thirteen*

## Hooray for Dollywood!

A long time ago, I wrote down
all the things I wanted out of life
and what I had to do to get them.

—Dolly Parton

In January 1986, Dolly Parton celebrated her
fortieth birthday. For many women, forty is the
time when youth slips away from them and middle age says hello. But not Dolly. She really had
something to celebrate in 1986; the best part of
her life was just beginning. She had never felt
better; her health problems seemed to be behind
her. Determined not to be fat and forty, she had
begun a new diet regimen that was working wonderfully. Her excess weight was literally melting

off, and she would begin 1987 some 50 pounds lighter.

She was at the top of her profession; Dolly's earnings were a reported $15,000,000 a year. She had set up a multimillion-dollar entertainment empire that many a male corporate executive would envy. The corporation she owned in common with Sandy Gallin, Sandollar, had recently signed a major film production deal with Universal Pictures. The first picture under discussion, to be scripted by Dolly, would reunite her with her favorite co-stars, Lily Tomlin and Jane Fonda. The film, tentatively titled *Brass Angels*, was, as they say in Hollywood, "in development."

Dolly's legal problems seemed to be over now. The $3,000,000 suit that Porter Wagoner had brought against her, the agony of which had sapped her emotional energies for years, was settled. Her other troublesome lawsuit had been dismissed.

In December 1985, the Grammy Award-winning "Nine to Five" made the front pages again, but this time in the most destructive way. The songwriting team of Neil and Jan Goldberg had accused Dolly Parton of plagiarism, of stealing the chorus of their song "Money World" and using it for "Nine to Five." In December, the case went to trial in Santa Monica, naming, as co-defendants along with Dolly, Jane Fonda and her husband, Tom Hayden. With celebrities like Dolly and Jane on the witness stand, the case never left the headlines or the 6 o'clock news for the 12 days during which it was heard. The jury deliberated for under an hour, and on December 20, it brought in a unanimous verdict for the defendants. Dolly Parton had won.

Three days later, the Goldbergs moved for a retrial, claiming that the jury was "starstruck" by Jane Fonda and Dolly Parton, and had reached its verdict against the weight of the evidence. The couple's request for a retrial was denied after a hearing in January 1986.

"That was so degrading," winced Dolly to her chronicler, Cliff Jahr, in the June 1986 *Ladies' Home Journal*. "One of the most painful things I've ever gone through. It damaged my reputation, I think, because there'll always be some people out there who think I would stoop so low as to steal from working people. Besides, there were only five musical notes in question, and they've been used in a hundred songs. The jury was out for twenty minutes, and we won. The court awarded me attorney's fees, which is a lot of money. Then the couple who sued me tried to get a retrial, claiming I charmed the jury because I played songs on the witness stand. The retrial was denied, and then they actually started trying to get me to record some of their songs."

There was irony involved here. Years before, Dolly had said in print that it was easier for her to do her own material because she didn't have time to go looking for songs. Also, listening to other people's material might always contain the possibility "that I might unconsciously take someone's tune." She didn't know then how her words would come back to haunt her later.

Dolly had released another hit album in the spring of 1985, *Real Love*, the title song for which she recorded as a duet with Kenny Rogers. The album cover showed a very different Dolly, a face that might have been photographed through a layer of Vaseline and eight layers of gauze, a shorter, less blatantly artificial wig, pale romantic colors, a white gown . . . a photograph shot *above* the chest. Who was this soft-focus apparition? Where were the gaudy sequins and the rhinestones? Nowhere to be seen. Dolly Parton was obviously classing up her image.

Dolly had just aired a second TV Christmas special—this time without Kenny Rogers—"A Smoky Mountain Christmas," which aired as the ABC Sunday Night Movie on December 14, 1985. With a flimsy plot dealing with seven orphans and one burned-out movie star (Dolly), it was a heart-wrencher starring Dolly Parton and Lee Majors, directed by Henry ("The Fonz") Winkler, and written by Dolly Parton. She also wrote six new songs for the special, including the title song, "A Smoky Mountain Christmas."

Dolly described the show as being "a combination of 'Snow White' and 'Sleeping Beauty,' " and hoped that it would become an annual TV event, and that the title song would become a Christmas classic, like "Jingle Bells." "Every songwriter dreams of writing a Christmas song that somebody's going to pick out and record."

Dolly had earned just about every honor the entertainment world could bestow, many of them more times than once. She now has a star of her own embedded in the Walk of the Stars on Hollywood Boulevard.

Creatively, Dolly is the author of some 3,000

songs, over 600 of which she has recorded. She owns enough platinum albums to start her own platinum mine.

Dolly Parton has bought or built homes in Nashville, a 6-bedroom house on Oahu, apartments and houses in Beverly Hills, Manhattan, and, recently, a large lakefront hideaway in Tennessee, this last one mostly for Carl to enjoy. By now she was making no secret of the fact that she and Carl Dean were sharing an open marriage, although she never revealed the names of her lovers. She had just about everything a woman could require to make her happy—youth, health, money, fame, the respect of her colleagues, and a great love life.

But *was* Dolly Parton completely fulfilled? Not yet.

There was a list of things she had sworn to do. There was always a list.

One was to get rid of some of the dead wood in her life. This she did periodically, and without mercy. It took a lot to make Dolly mad, but once she got mad, she was implacable. With her customary mysteriousness, the mystery that Jane Fonda had remarked upon, Dolly will not say who that dead wood was, but admits that she sat down and wrote a series of letters, severing some business and some family ties, and that took care of that.

"Y'know what I did?" she asked Cliff Jahr in his June 1986 interview in *Ladies' Home Journal*. "I got up early and went straight to a list of names I'd made. I wrote letters to four people, some family, some business, who I had let mess with my head. They're people who's had the upper hand on me for years. When I saw them comin', I'd cringe. When they called, I wasn't in.

"The letters were very blunt. They said: 'I'm not going to put up with your B.S. anymore. You have no control over me, and little control of yourself, so you should examine things very carefully.' Then I made some phone calls, too. I decided to get all the grief and worries over irresponsible people out of my life. And it worked—it really cleared the air."

The next thing on Dolly's list was Dollywood.

A decade earlier, when she was interviewed by Barbara Walters on Barbara's TV special, Dolly had confessed that she wanted to build a fantasy world somewhere in the mountains for everybody to share with her. It was an ambition Dolly Parton was to talk about wistfully over and over throughout the years when she was becoming successful. She also said, again and again, that her dream was for people to be able to see just what her part of the country was really like, how her people really lived. Too, it was an important part of Dolly's ambition to pump money back into her rural east Tennessee, bring in the tourists with their open pocketbooks, and create jobs for local people.

In 1986, Dolly Parton's threefold ambitious dream came to pass at last.

Dollywood was by no means a unique concept. In 1948, Roy Acuff opened his Dunbar Cave resort near Clarksville, Tennessee. Among the other famous country artists who have their own museums or theme parks are: Conway Twitty with

Twitty City; Barbara Mandrell and Mandrell Country; Jimmie Rodgers; Minnie Pearl; Roy Rogers, who houses a stuffed and frighteningly lifelike Trigger in his Roy Rogers Museum; Lorretta Lynn's Hurricane Mills dude ranch; Jim Reeves; Hank Williams, Jr., and his Kawliga Corners; Merle Haggard's Silverthorn fishing resort; Waylon Jennings; the House of Cash owned by Johnny Cash—the list goes on. Not to mention the most famous hillbilly Disneyland of them all, Graceland, which was Elvis Presley's home when he was alive, and a multimillion-dollar money-coiner after his death. Tourists flock there to the tune of 500,000 visitors a year.

It's not the price of admission alone that brings the gold tumbling into the coffers; it's the souvenirs, the fast foods, the rides, the price of film and the photo developing, the bumper stickers, the motel accommodations—all adding up to tourist dollars in the millions. Naturally, when Dolly Parton decided to open her own amusement park, it had to be the biggest and the best. Fighting off the leering wags who suggested she call her project Titty City, Dolly opted for Dollywood. "It just popped into my mind that it would be a good name for a park."

When Dolly made up her mind to build the biggest and best theme park of any of the country music stars, and bring business flowing into her part of Tennessee, she didn't have to start from scratch. There was an already existing historical-theme amusement park on Route 441 at Pigeon Forge, first known as Gold Rush Park, later as Silver Dollar City. Why compete? Why not simply join forces and expand? Accordingly, the Parton organization joined hands with Jack Herschend, who founded Silver Dollar City, and thus was born Dollywood (in the logo, the "W" is a butterfly with wings spread), now called "A Silver Dollar City Theme Park," which is a 400-acre spread located 30 miles south of Knoxville, in the foothills of, and gateway to, the Great Smoky Mountains, where Dolly grew up. The new park has 50 percent more acreage than Silver Dollar City had.

In July 1985, Dolly returned to Sevierville to put the plan for Dollywood in front of the city council and get its financial support. The city kicked in $600,000 and the state of Tennessee $1,600,000, to update the streets, the lighting, the sewer system, and other amenities in and around the proposed expansion. The newly cosmeticized and updated park is a $20,000,000 venture in which Dolly's and her partner's investment is said to be around $6,000,000. The park opened in a blizzard of publicity on May 3, 1986.

Dolly's personal part of the park is Daydream Ridge, which has been built to resemble rural Tennessee sometime before the turn of the century. In a craftsmen's village are to be seen local Tennessee artisans creating the homespun crafts of yesteryear: sewing quilts, carving wood, making wagons, blowing glass, and shoeing horses, all before tourists' eyes.

Dollywood offers, among other treats and the obligatory thrill rides, a rags-to-riches tour of Dolly's life, in the Dolly Parton Story Museum, which contains many of her costumes and wigs, gold

records, guitars, photos, and other Parton memora-
bilia. There's Rivertown Junction, which has
restaurants like Aunt Granny's Dixie Fixin's (her
many nieces and nephews call Dolly "Aunt
Granny"), and Apple Jack's cider press and mill,
which serves apples in more ways than one wants
to know about.

Dollywood boasts a Nine to Five and Dime
Mercantile, and a gift shop that can't be passed
up—The Parton Back Porch Theater, which is a
copy of her old back porch, but which is now an
outdoor concert stage with 700 seats. Dolly hired
her sister Stella, herself something of a country
music star, to stage country music concerts, along
with her brother Randy and her sister Frieda, and
her Uncle Bill Owens, all alumni of the Travelin'
Family Band.

There is also white-water rafting on The Smoky
Mountain Rampage, a miniature railroad called
The Dollywood Express, and a lot more. The park
offers mountain crafts, bluegrass festivals, restaurants where visitors can stuff their faces with
Dolly's "favorite foods," such as apple fritters,
banana pudding, funnel cakes, hickory-smoked
meats, Mountain Burgers, and more.

Nobody goes away without visiting the replica
of her 2-room Tennessee Mountain Home, complete down to the spittoon, and bearing a plaque
in front that reads: "These mountains and my
childhood home have a special place in my heart.
They inspire my music and my life. I hope being
here does the same for you."

"Dollywood is not about Dolly Parton," she
said. "It never once crossed my mind that it was

an ego trip. It's about Smoky Mountain people and their way of life. These are my people and I was in a position to do something great for them. Dollywood has provided a lot of jobs and rejuvenated a lot of pride my people have in their heritage. People in New York and Los Angeles may not know it, but Smoky Mountain National Park is one of the most visited national parks in the country [9,000,000 visitors a year]. I knew all we had to do was put Dollywood right in the middle of all that traffic, then get ourselves some publicity. I knew it would work. We had one and a half million people the first year. Now we're expanding to accommodate even more the second. I'm going to make some good money, too. I may be a country bumpkin, but I'm a smart country bumpkin."

Even as Dolly Parton was crossing Dollywood off her list of Things to Do Today, another item on the list, an item already ten years old, was coming into fruition.

In its March 23, 1978, issue, Rolling Stone ran an item headlined "Ronstadt, Parton, and Harris's Secret Project." The story said that three of the hottest women singers in the business—Linda Ronstadt, Emmylou Harris, and Dolly Parton—were recording an album together, and had sworn one another to a secrecy "worthy of the Manhattan Project [which yielded the atomic bomb]." Because the three singers were signed to different record labels, it was a difficult deal to work out, but it was agreed that Asylum, Linda Ronstadt's label, should release the album, and tentative plans were made to set up a group of charity concerts

when the album was completed. That was in
1978.

Dolly Parton met Linda Ronstadt at the "Grand
Ole Opry" more than 12 years ago, and they became friends. In 1974, Linda and Emmylou Harris had cut a country song together, "I Can't Help
It If I'm Still in Love with You," and it went to
number one on the country music chart.

Nineteen seventy-four was a crossover year for
Linda Ronstadt, the singer from Tucson, Arizona.
That was when Linda, queen of the "L.A. country-
rock set," spanned both the pop and the country
charts with her classic *Heart Like a Wheel* album.
Her Nashville album was *Silk Purse*, containing
the beautiful ballad "Long Long Time."

From her crossover into country in 1974, Linda
Ronstadt began to have one platinum award-
winning album after another: *Heart Like a Wheel;
Prisoner in Disguise; Hasten Down the Wind; Linda
Ronstadt's Greatest Hits; Living in the U.S.A.* The
list is virtually endless, like Dolly's own catalog
of hits. And, just like Dolly Parton, Linda Ronstadt
drew her fans from a cross-section of the record-
buying population, crossing age, gender, and re-
gional barriers.

As for Emmylou Harris, she is one of the most
admired and respected country music singers; her
voice is pure country. As *Country Music* magazine said about her in 1984, "With her crystalline
voice, her rhapsodic beauty, her plaintive emot-
ing, her winsome onstage shyness, her delicate
wholesomeness combined with a sort of freewheel-
ing rambunctiousness, Emmylou has inspired

something almost like worship among her follow-
ers."

Dolly respected them both; they respected each
other and Dolly, especially as a composer. Both
Linda and Emmylou had recorded Dolly Parton
songs; Emmylou Harris's version of "Coat of Many
Colors" is enough to make a stone weep. So,
when the three women got together for the first
time in Emmylou Harris's Los Angeles home,
magic began to happen.

"We just got a guitar and sang 'When I Stopped
Dreaming,' " says Emmylou. "Then we sang the
Christmas song 'Light of the Stable' to an acoustic
guitar. And it sounded so good, I asked the other
two, 'If I record "Light of the Stable," will you
come and sing with me on the track?' And they
both said yes. So it was natural that we sort of
went on from there."

Said Dolly on "The Oprah Winfrey Show" in
the spring of 1987, "The three of us became friends
about twelve or thirteen years ago, and the first
time we were together we were in Emmylou Harris's living room, and we just started to sing some
of the old gospel songs and country songs, and
we said, boy! This sounds good! It was the kind
of harmony that usually just family can get. You
know how in family if you sing there is a certain
blend. We thought we sounded like sisters and
we should record it. We tried it almost ten years
ago, and it didn't come together then because
there was so much pressure on us. The labels
were telling us to do this, do that, do some rock
'n' roll, do some country. We just decided that
what we had in our minds was too good to be

wasted on so much frustration, so we put it on the shelf. Every time we'd get together through the years, we'd say, 'We just got to record this album.' So this past year, Linda called me and Emmylou and said, 'Let's make the time,' so we did."

They began recording on Dolly's birthday, and this time the *Trio* album came together as though it had always just been there, waiting to be set free into the world. Said Dolly of the album, "I know it took forever to make, but we just love it. It's real country, acoustic, and very down-home. Emmy sounds so good. And no one can sing a rock or country song like Linda."

Is it possible that an album of pure country singing by three of the most famous and most beautiful voices in country music could fail? No.

It didn't.

Is it possible that such an album as *Trio* wouldn't head directly for the top of the charts and stay there? No.

It did. At this writing, it is still at the top of the charts.

When the feminist *Ms.* magazine released its list of Women of the Year at the end of 1986, Dolly Parton's name was on it. She was honored for "creating popular songs about real women," and "for bringing jobs and understanding to the mountain people of Tennessee."

Gloria Steinem herself, one of the founding editors of *Ms.* and the personification of American feminism, wrote about Dolly: "She has crossed musical class lines to bring work, real life, and strong women into a world of pop usually dominated by unreal romance. She has used her business sense to bring other women and poor people along with her. And her flamboyant style has turned all the devalued symbols of womanliness to her own ends. If feminism means each of us finding our unique power, and helping other women do the same, Dolly Parton certainly has done both.''

Nineteen eighty-seven was the year Dolly left RCA Records and signed with CBS Records. "It was like an old marriage," she explained. "We'd begun to take each other for granted a little bit. What I needed was a fresh start, and some real success in my recording career. With this new deal at CBS, I'm going to do one great authentic country album every year, and one pop album. No more mixin' them up and tryin' to please everybody all at the same time."

As though Dollywood, Trio, a new slimmer figure, a new recording contract, validation by the feminist movement, and a new lease on life weren't enough goodies for Dolly to find in her Christmas stocking, 1987 brought Dolly Parton another piece of something wonderful—a $40,000,000 contract with her production company for her own ABC-TV 60-minute variety series, "The Dolly Show," to debut in the fall of 1987.

"It's goin' to be a tough battle—there are some really great shows to beat—but we're going to come out on top," she promises. "If you think you've seen a TV variety show before, forget it— you ain't seen nothin' yet. Variety has been off too long, and I have a lot more talent than people realize."

Even though there has not been a successful variety show on television in ten years, not since the Barbara Mandrell series, the ABC network has committed to two full seasons of the specials at $1,000,000 per show. Brandon Stoddard, president of ABC's entertainment division, says, "There are few stars in the world who have the instant recognition and sheer likability of Dolly Parton, and to say we are delighted that she will be part of our weekly series lineup this fall is the understatement of the season."

Sandy Gallin, Dolly's partner, is producing the program. "She wants to utilize her talents," he said. "Dolly doesn't want to sit around waiting for the perfect movie script to come in. She feels she is a performing talent and should be in front of an audience entertaining people. What better platform to do that than a weekly variety show?"

Dolly is planning a "lot of surprises" that will make the show different from any others, and she bets it will run at least five years.

With Dolly Parton at the helm, who can doubt it? The ten-year-old hillbilly girl who stood up and sang to her first TV audience at 5:30 in the morning over WIVK in Knoxville grew up to become the forty-one-year-old woman who is one of the world's greatest entertainers, not just a superstar but a megastar. The girl who left the mountains to see the big wide world has introduced millions of people to an understanding of those mountains.

Anybody who can do that can do anything.

# *Epilogue*

## Here I Come Again

I'm Dolly Parton from the mountains, and that's what I'll remain.

—Dolly Parton

The importance of music in Dolly's life cannot be overemphasized. Music is her best friend, her deepest and longest-held love, her chosen companion. Movies and television are wonderful, but they will never take the place of Dolly Parton's music. It is her strongest commitment. Above all, she thinks of herself as a songwriter. She writes anywhere, everywhere, getting up in the middle of the night to do it, interrupting a meal in a restaurant to jot down lyrics or titles on paper napkins and matchbooks. When she is writing a song, she forgets everything else in the world.

"I'm a songwriter first, a singer and performer second. I want to be known as a great writer—now, that's a dream of mine. I would describe my writing as being simply complicated. It's got enough depth to be appreciated, and enough simplicity to be understood. Everybody wants to be successful at whatever their inner dream is. I'm not near finished with what I want to do, with what I want to accomplish yet. I want to be somebody that left behind something good and beautiful for somebody else to enjoy."

Dolly once said to Kip Kirby, "Music is my personal addiction. So much of everything I've done has only been to open more doors for the music itself. It all gets back to the fact that I am, first of all, a songwriter and a singer."

Dolly has been known to write as many as 20 songs in one day. She has "thousands more" either already down on paper or in her head.

When interviewed on "The Oprah Winfrey Show," Dolly demonstrated how she used her very long artificial nails as a musical instrument, clicking them together in rhythm. Sometimes, when she is without her guitar, and a scrap of music enters her head, she will use her fingernails to capture it before she can get somebody to write it down. She still can't read a note of music.

As for the future of her open marriage to Carl Dean, it is difficult to see it ever coming to an end. Why should it, when it allows Dolly so much freedom, and at the same time so much support? Ten years ago, Dolly said to Barbara

Walters about her husband, "He's the kind of person that if bein' apart, if I should meet somebody, I would never tell Carl. He would never know and I would never tell him. And it wouldn't hurt him. It's the same way with him. I wouldn't want to know it. As long as he loves me and as long as he's good to me and as long as we're good to each other. I don't think it happens, but I'm just sayin' I wouldn't want to pry in it.

"My husband is a very home-based type of person. He's very moral and the most unselfish person I've ever known. He's very deep and very witty. He's good for me because he's so different in nature from me. There's nobody else like him and I know in my heart that there will never be another person for me. I just know it."

She has often said, "Carl's not a jealous person and neither am I. He understands that music is so much a part of me and he understands that I couldn't be happy without my music, as much as I love him. There would be so much of me missing, I wouldn't be myself. He's the one man in my life, and I want to grow old with him. If he should die first, I'd probably never marry again. That's how deep my love for him is."

Dolly's country wit is celebrated, and it's often been turned against herself. "I'm six-foot-four in heels." "I don't look this way out of ignorance. If people think that I do, they're dumber than I am." She also has a tendency to speak of herself in the third person—"Dolly does this," or "Dolly does that." She has talked about the possibility of "Dolly changing her look."

"If I felt strongly enough about the character I

was going to play, I wouldn't mind changing my look. Eventually, that will be one of my challenges, to be another personality."

It would seem that Dolly Parton has in fact recently changed her look. She is so thin now that she has an odd birdlike appearance. Her breasts, while certainly smaller than they were when she was 50 pounds heavier, are still the largest part of her body. Her waist is 17 or 18 inches around, but her chest measurement can't be less than 38 or 39 inches. She dresses far more modestly, even turning up in tailored costumes that outline her brand-new figure. Is the old gaudy, spangle-loving Dolly Parton gone for good?

There is even some trepidation among her friends (and in the supermarket tabloids) that Dolly may have gone *too* far with this weight-reduction regimen of hers. She is down to a perfect size, and weighs no more than 100 pounds, but still she continues to diet. Is she a borderline anorexic, or has she crossed that border? Or is she the victim of an eating disorder that will make her thin, then fat, then thin again, then fat once more, for the rest of her life? Dolly Parton is a person who takes control, and this is one vital area she certainly must watch.

Ten years ago, in Chet Flippo's cover interview with Dolly for *Rolling Stone*, she told him, "There is no top and no bottom to my career because once I accomplish the things I decide I'm going to, then I want to get into other things. I am a list maker. I like to write my goals and plans down and keep them in a secret place where people can't see them. You'd be *amazed* that even *years* ago the things I'd written down on my list, that I just mark 'em off as they come true and I think, boy, if *that* ain't proof that positive thinkin' is a marvelous thing. I practiced that all my life; *that's* what got me out of the mountains. Even as a little child, I daydreamed *so* strongly that I just saw these things happen and, sure enough, they would. We can be whatever we want to be, the Bible says that, that *all* things are possible, and it says that if you have faith even as a grain of mustard seed, then you shall move mountains and that nothing shall be impossible unto you."

So far, nothing seems to have been impossible unto Dolly Parton. What does the future hold? More of the same? A climb to even greater heights?

"Every seven years I sit down and make a new plan."

Among the new plans Dolly is making these days, besides her total involvement in her new ABC-TV variety show, are: a line of diet foods called Slim Pickin's at the same time that she wants to open a chain of restaurants to sell heavy, greasy country food like biscuits and gravy, fatback and greens—Aunt Granny's; a line of cosmetics—Dollyface; that motion picture which is to reunite Dolly, Lily, and Jane, but for which no final script has been approved. Will this take longer than Linda, Emmylou, and Dolly getting together to record *Trio*?; a Broadway musical about her life in east Tennessee, *Wildflowers*; self-help and inspirational books under her contract with Simon & Schuster; footwear, lingerie, songs, albums, the possibility of a tour with Emmylou Harris and Linda Ronstadt. Dolly Parton has enough irons in the fire to burn down a good-sized cabin.

What about this: Dolly Parton for President of the United States? Don't laugh. America laughed at the thought of Ronald Reagan. With Dolly as President, the budget would balance, we would be at peace with the rest of the world, and every day would start with a song. Besides, Dolly Parton has a rare integrity, matched with inner strength and a core of steel; she says that, while she never learned to harden her heart, she has learned to strengthen the muscles around it. She fasts and prays before every major decision. We should have more, much more, of that quality in our world leaders.

Dolly Parton's not afraid of growing old.

"I'll be a great old lady, lots of fun and busy and smarter," she told Cliff Jahr, "full of life and still foolin' around a little. If it's God's will that I'm healthy and I keep my mind, I can always sing, write for other people, manage, produce, do a talk show, a variety show, a TV series. I get these incredible offers all the time, but during this part of my career, I'm going for the bigger stuff—the movies, Dollywood, books I'm going to write, and helping to run my new film and TV production companies with my manager.

"I don't want people to think of me as someone who has not tasted enough of life to be an artist. I've had a *full* meal.

"When I sit back in my rocking chair some-day," Dolly Parton says, smiling, "I want to be able to say I've done it all."

# STAR BOOKS BESTSELLERS

| | | |
|---|---|---|
| 0352315520 | **TESSA BARCLAY**<br>**Garland of War** | £1.95 |
| 0352317612 | **The Wine Widow** | £2.50 |
| 0352304251 | **A Sower Went Forth** | £2.25 |
| 0352308060 | **The Stony Places** | £2.25 |
| 0352313331 | **Harvest of Thorns** | £2.25 |
| 0352315857 | **The Good Ground** | £1.95 |
| 035231687X | **Champagne Girls** | £2.95 |
| 0352316969 | **JOANNA BARNES**<br>**Silverwood** | £3.25 |
| 035231270X | **LOIS BATTLE**<br>**War Brides** | £2.75* |
| 0352316640 | **Southern Women** | £2.95* |

*STAR Books are obtainable from many booksellers and newsagents. If you have any difficulty tick the titles you want and fill in the form below.*

Name _____

Address _____

_____

Send to: Star Books Cash Sales, P.O. Box 11, Falmouth, Cornwall, TR10 9EN.

Please send a cheque or postal order to the value of the cover price plus:
 UK: 55p for the first book, 22p for the second book and 14p for each additional book ordered to the maximum charge of £1.75.

BFPO and EIRE: 55p for the first book, 22p for the second book, 14p per copy for the next 7 books, thereafter 8p per book.

OVERSEAS: £1.00 for the first book and 25p per copy for each additional book.

*While every effort is made to keep prices low, it is sometimes necessary to increase prices at short notice. Star Books reserve the right to show new retail prices on covers which may differ from those advertised in the text or elsewhere.*

**NOT FOR SALE IN CANADA*

# STAR BOOKS BESTSELLERS

| | | |
|---|---|---|
| | MICHAEL CARSON | |
| 0352316179 | **The Genesis Experiement** | £2.50 |
| | ASHLEY CARTER | |
| 035231 7264 | **A Darkling Moon** | £2.50* |
| 035231639X | **Embrace The Wind** | £2.25* |
| 0352315717 | **Farewell to Blackoaks** | £1.95* |
| 0352316365 | **Miz Lucretia of Falconhurst** | £2.50* |
| | ASHLEY CARTER & KYLE ONSTOTT | |
| 0352317019 | **Strange Harvest** | £2.95* |
| | BERNARD F. CONNERS | |
| 0352315814 | **Don't Embarrass The Bureau** | £1.95* |
| 0352314362 | **Dancehall** | £2.25* |

*STAR Books are obtainable from many booksellers and newsagents. If you have any difficulty tick the titles you want and fill in the form below.*

Name _____

Address _____

_____

Send to: Star Books Cash Sales, P.O. Box 11, Falmouth, Cornwall, TR10 9EN.

Please send a cheque or postal order to the value of the cover price plus:
UK: 55p for the first book, 22p for the second book and 14p for each additional book ordered to the maximum charge of £1.75.

BFPO and EIRE: 55p for the first book, 22p for the second book, 14p per copy for the next 7 books, thereafter 8p per book.

OVERSEAS: £1.00 for the first book and 25p per copy for each additional book.

*While every effort is made to keep prices low, it is sometimes necessary to increase prices at short notice. Star Books reserve the right to show new retail prices on covers which may differ from those advertised in the text or elsewhere.*

*NOT FOR SALE IN CANADA

# STAR BOOKS BESTSELLERS

| | | |
|---|---|---|
| | **CATHERINE COOKSON** | |
| 0426163524 | **Hannah Massey** | £1.95 |
| 0352311339 | **The Garment** | £1.95 |
| 0426163605 | **Slinky Jane** | £1.95 |
| | **HENRY DENKER** | |
| 0352309601 | **Horowitz and Mrs Washington** | £2.50* |
| 0352303522 | **The Experiment** | £1.95* |
| 0352396067 | **The Physicians** | £1.95* |
| 0352312947 | **Outrage** | £1.95* |
| 0352316446 | **Kate Kincaid** | £2.95* |
| | **SUSANNAH CURTIS** | |
| 0352318376 | **The Sad and Happy Years** | £2.95 |
| | **REGINE DEFORGES** | |
| 0352317930 | **The Blue Bicycle** | £2.95 |

*STAR Books are obtainable from many booksellers and newsagents. If you have any difficulty tick the titles you want and fill in the form below.*

Name _____

Address _____

_____

_____

**Send to: Star Books Cash Sales, P.O. Box 11, Falmouth, Cornwall, TR10 9EN.**

**Please send a cheque or postal order to the value of the cover price plus:**
 UK: 55p for the first book, 22p for the second book and 14p for each additional book ordered to the maximum charge of £1.75.

**BFPO and EIRE:** 55p for the first book, 22p for the second book, 14p per copy for the next 7 books, thereafter 8p per book.

**OVERSEAS:** £1.00 for the first book and 25p per copy for each additional book.

*While every effort is made to keep prices low, it is sometimes necessary to increase prices at short notice. Star Books reserve the right to show new retail prices on covers which may differ from those advertised in the text or elsewhere.*

*NOT FOR SALE IN CANADA

# STAR BOOKS BESTSELLERS

| | **THOMAS FLEMING** | |
|---|---|---|
| 0352316950 | **The Spoils of War** | £3.95* |
| 0352313986 | **Dreams of Glory** | £2.95* |
| 0352312750 | **Promises to Keep** | £3.25* |
| 0352310634 | **The Officers' Wives** | £3.95* |
| | **DORIS FLOOD LADD** | |
| 0352316977 | **The Irish** | £2.95* |
| | **ANDREW M. GREELEY** | |
| 0352311010 | **The Cardinal Sins** | £1.95* |
| 0352312459 | **Thy Brother's Wife** | £1.95* |
| 0352314354 | **Ascent into Hell** | £1.95* |
| 0352315733 | **Lord of the Dance** | £2.50* |

*STAR Books are obtainable from many booksellers and newsagents. If you have any difficulty tick the titles you want and fill in the form below.*

Name _____

Address _____

_____

Send to: Star Books Cash Sales, P.O. Box 11, Falmouth, Cornwall, TR10 9EN.

Please send a cheque or postal order to the value of the cover price plus: UK: 55p for the first book, 22p for the second book and 14p for each additional book ordered to the maximum charge of £1.75.

BFPO and EIRE: 55p for the first book, 22p for the second book, 14p per copy for the next 7 books, thereafter 8p per book.

OVERSEAS: £1.00 for the first book and 25p per copy for each additional book.

*While every effort is made to keep prices low, it is sometimes necessary to increase prices at short notice. Star Books reserve the right to show new retail prices on covers which may differ from those advertised in the text or elsewhere.*

**\*NOT FOR SALE IN CANADA**

# STAR BOOKS BESTSELLERS

*STAR Books are obtainable from many booksellers and newsagents. If you have any difficulty tick the titles you want and fill in the form below.*

Name _____

Address _____

_____

Send to: Star Books Cash Sales, P.O. Box 11, Falmouth, Cornwall, TR10 9EN.

**Please** send a cheque or postal order to the value of the cover price plus:
UK: 55p for the first book, 22p for the second book and 14p for each additional book ordered to the maximum charge of £1.75.
BFPO and EIRE: 55p for the first book, 22p for the second book, 14p per copy for the next 7 books, thereafter 8p per book.
OVERSEAS: £1.00 for the first book and 25p per copy for each additional book.

*While every effort is made to keep prices low, it is sometimes necessary to increase prices at short notice. Star Books reserve the right to show new retail prices on covers which may differ from those advertised in the text or elsewhere.*

*NOT FOR SALE IN CANADA

# STAR BOOKS BESTSELLERS

| | FRANÇOISE SAGAN | |
|---|---|---|
| 0352314834 | **The Painted Lady** | £2.25* |
| 035231611X | **The Still Storm** | £1.95* |
| 035231690X | **The Unmade Bed** | £2.25* |
| 0352317272 | **Incidental Music** | £2.00* |
| 0352317914 | **Le Chien Couchant** | £1.95* |
| | RICHARD BEN SAPIR | |
| 0352315121 | **The Body** | £2.50* |
| 0352316748 | **Bressio** | £2.50* |
| 0352315970 | **Spies** | £2.50* |
| | STANLEY SHAW **Sherlock Holmes at the** | |
| 0362315903 | **1902 Fifth Test** | £1.95 |
| | IRENE SHUBIK | |
| 0352319941 | **The War Guest** | £1.95 |

*STAR Books are obtainable from many booksellers and newsagents. If you have any difficulty tick the titles you want and fill in the form below.*

Name _____

Address _____

_____

Send to: Star Books Cash Sales, P.O. Box 11, Falmouth, Cornwall, TR10 9EN.

Please send a cheque or postal order to the value of the cover price plus: UK: 55p for the first book, 22p for the second book and 14p for each additional book ordered to the maximum charge of £1.75.

BFPO and EIRE: 55p for the first book, 22p for the second book, 14p per copy for the next 7 books, thereafter 8p per book.

OVERSEAS: £1.00 for the first book and 25p per copy for each additional book.

*While every effort is made to keep prices low, it is sometimes necessary to increase prices at short notice. Star Books reserve the right to show new retail prices on covers which may differ from those advertised in the text or elsewhere.*

*NOT FOR SALE IN CANADA